THE
SOCIOLOGY
OF
DEVELOPMENT

Aidan Foster-Carter

Causeway Books

British Library Cataloguing in Publication Data

Foster-Carter, Aidan
    The sociology of development.—(Themes and
perspectives in sociology)
    1. Community development—Developing countries
    2. Developing countries—Social conditions
    I. Title   II. Series
    307'.14'091724   HN980

    ISBN 0-946183-08-2

Causeway Press Ltd.
PO Box 13, Ormskirk, Lancashire L39 5HP
©Causeway Press Ltd., 1985

Production by BPMS, Ormskirk.
Typesetting by Bookform, Merseyside
Printed and bound in England
by Hartnoll Print, Bodmin, Cornwall

Contents

Chapter Seven

Chapter Eight

Chapter Nine

Women and Development

Chapter Ten

Religion

Bibliography

Index

Preface

Acknowledgements

Writing a short introductory book has inevitably made me dependent on earlier labourers in the same vineyard. To avoid endless footnoting in the text, let me express here my gratitude to the authors of the more substantial textbooks which you should read next: especially Hardiman and Midgley, and my colleague and friend John E. Goldthorpe. The Open University course in *Third World Studies* (U204) contains far and away the best integrated materials on development, including a marvellous *Atlas*; every school and college should have a set.

Academically, I have the usual debts from twenty years of learning and (maybe) teaching. So, anonymous thanks to all (you know who you are), in Oxford and Hull, Dar es Salaam and Leeds; not to mention Africa and the Caribbean, the USA, Turkey and East Asia.

Finally, and by no means anonymously, there are the indispensable midwives of my labour. My mother, Ethna Foster-Carter, provided rural peace and sustenance in deepest wintry Hampshire while I did most of the writing. Without her and without that, I doubt if the book would have materialized at all. Margaret Gothelf, Lyn Kelly, Gena Lodge and Carol Peaker all typed, somehow, as they always do, my handwriting which Gets No Better. I owe them a lot. And Mike Haralambos, whose special mission in life is getting academic sociologists off their butts to produce that which they have it in them to write, had an even harder task than usual with me. Although I've spent most of the past year and more wishing he'd never asked, at the end of the day I'm profoundly grateful.

The book is dedicated to Olivia.

Author's biases

Although an author shouldn't ram herself down the reader's throat, neither should her 'Author-ity' go unquestioned. I have at least three biases which you should be aware of. One is by *region*. The Third World that I know is mostly Africa and East Asia, rather than (say) Latin America or South Asia. Then there is *ideological* bias. Being of the 'class of 1968', I was much influenced by Marxism – an influence I don't regret, although I'm no longer a Marxist. Hence, in terms of this book, my sympathies are more with the 'dependency' than the 'modernization' approach to development – although naturally I've tried to be fair to both. Thirdly, I used to be a real *theory* freak; but that's changing (writing this book has helped), and I'm glad. Theory is fine if (and only if) it's put to work. Maybe this is empiricism, moving to the right, and/or old age. Anyway, you have been warned . . .

Aim of this book

This book is just a long essay, a taster really: hopelessly ambitious in trying to cover far too much ground. It is, at best, an *introduction*. Perhaps it's natural for people who write about the Third World to have a bit of a missionary impulse; but I really believe the sociology of development is the most fascinating and crucial area of all. So I shall be well enough pleased if this book excites your curiosity enough to make you want to go on and do some serious reading on the subject. If it doesn't, I've failed.

Chapter One

Sociology and Development

Introduction

The sociology of development is an unusual kind of 'specialism' –
and hard to cram into a short book. First, this 'specialism' is actually
the study of most of the world! Conversely, the 'general' sociology you
learn is in reality about that minority who live in 'Western' societies.
So often, Western sociologists generalize about urbanism, industrialism, education, the family, etc; ignoring the fact that *most* people
actually live in the Third World, in rather different *kinds* of cities (or
not in cities), undergoing very different *forms* of industrialization (if
any), with a wide variety of education systems, family structures, etc.
So really it's the sociology of development which should include all the
rest of sociology, rather than the other way round!

However, and secondly, the sociology of development includes more
than sociology alone. It has to be *interdisciplinary*. You can't just leave
out (say) politics or economics. Otherwise you end up with what's been
called the 'underlabourer' notion of sociology – a sort of cringing
hyena, waiting in the shadows while the fat cats of economics and
politics take the meat, before sidling up to the carcass for whatever
pickings are left: religion, the family, etc. I don't mean that these
pickings are unimportant, obviously. But they really are not the whole
body of the subject, and a diet confined to them would be seriously
unbalanced.

Anyway, all social reality is in some sense a seamless robe, and disci-
plinary divisions are arbitrary. The founders of sociology, notably Karl
Marx and Max Weber, certainly tackled economic and political issues
in a sociological way. And one particular reason for doing this in our
field is that in development we simply don't know (or people don't

agree) what *is* the key dimension. Is it economic factors, or political, or social, or even psychological ones, which advance or hold back the development of societies? I hope you can see why it would be wrong to define the subject in such a way as to rule out any of these in advance.

Thirdly, there is an important but boring point which I shall stress only this once – though it applies to every sentence in this book. The Third World – the object of the sociology of development – is not homogeneous. On the contrary, it is highly *diverse*. It consists of three or four continents, each containing dozens of different countries and hundreds of once separate cultures. How on earth can we dare to generalize about all that? 'With great care' is the only possible answer. So, although this short book inevitably contains many generalizations, there will always be somewhere to which a particular point doesn't apply. (And besides, somebody else might read the balance of the evidence differently.)

Nonetheless – and this is my fourth introductory point – there have been two main perspectives in the sociology of development which *have* tried to generalize about the Third World. Usually known as *modernization theory* and *dependency theory*, they are dealt with in subsequent chapters. As adversaries, giving very different accounts of why the Third World is underdeveloped, these two schools have often clashed in heated debate. In this book, however, besides assessing them as theory, I make a conscious attempt to pull these two old war-horses off the jousting field, put saddle and harness on them, and see if they can still carry a load. To be precise, the substantive chapters – on industrialization, urbanism, education, health, etc. – try to concretize the arguments of the theory chapter, and assess which (if either) of the two perspectives best helps us understand what's actually going on in the Third World in these particular areas.

Terms and Definitions

Development/Underdevelopment. This book's title is *The Sociology of Development*. But what does 'development' *mean*? Some of the overtones are obvious: a sense of *process*, and more than that of *progress*. But *what* process? and what *is* progress? On such matters there is no agreement.

We may make progress, however, by looking at two or three arguably related themes. Not the least of the problems of the sociology of development is how, if at all, it relates to other areas of sociology. One obvious candidate for a predecessor is *social evolutionism*: pioneered by Comte and Spencer, and still persisting (or revived) in parts of the later work of Talcott Parsons. What is interesting here is the idea of societies as developing through a *fixed series of stages*, in a definite order.

But should we think of *societies* in such terms? Probably the simplest way I can introduce to you the first major school in the sociology of development, *modernization theory*, is to say that on the whole this *is* how they think about social development: as proceeding through certain stages, in a fixed order. On this basis, we can think of the world as a kind of continuum, with different 'societies' (which by now probably means nation-states, although it didn't always) ranged at various points along what is claimed to be the same route. Latecomers follow in the footsteps of pioneers. As Marx said, the more developed society thus shows to the less developed the image of its own future. One contemporary modernization theorist who explicitly thinks along these lines is *Walt Rostow*, whose 'stages of economic growth' we shall consider in the next chapter.

Such a view gives us a vocabulary, and a particular way of using it. Countries which have made it, or are far along, are *developed* (which doesn't imply that they've stopped, but rather that they're over the hump – or, in Rostow's famous metaphor, the 'take-off'). Conversely, there are other as yet *less developed countries* (often abbreviated to LDCs). These may also be called – optimistically, and in a sense begging the question – *developing countries*. Yet a third term for the same thing, seemingly more neutral, is *underdeveloped* – first used in this sense in the 1940s.

However, according to *dependency theory*, the second major school in the sociology of development, this whole terminology is by no means neutral. From their very different standpoint, and as one of them (André Gunder Frank) put it, *under*development is not at all the same as *un*development. If by the latter we mean a relative lack of development (such as we may presume to have been the lot of Europe too in pre-capitalist or pre-industrial times), this is *not* the same as what prevails in the Third World (see below!) today. For, according to dependency theory, evolutionist assumptions are quite inappropriate. Underdevelopment, far from being a stage on the way to development, is a totally different situation – on a road that leads nowhere. And this in turn is because it is not (or not only) a process, but a *relation*: it is something (something not very nice, either) which someone has done to somebody else.

Hence Gunder Frank, like a guerilla capturing an enemy's gun, takes the word 'underdevelop' and turns it around – as seen in the title of another classic dependency work, Walter Rodney's *How Europe*

Underdeveloped Africa (1972). Underdevelopment, on this view, involves imperialism and exploitation. Third World societies have been prevented from developing because this serves the interest of the West.

As yet, I make no comments on the relative merits of modernization and dependency theories: that task comes later. For now, you should just be aware of their overlapping vocabularies which nonetheless mean very different things.

First/Second/Third World. 'Third World' (we shall come back to First and Second) is widely used in practice as a synonym for developing coutries or less developed countries (LDCs). However, its implications are somewhat different, in two ways. First, it was an attempt to get away from 'Cold War' assumptions that the entire world was divided into only two power blocs, West and East, headed by the USA and USSR. Second, 'Third World' was a *self-conscious* grouping, one possessing awareness of its own identity. (To adapt what Marx says about class: a group *for* itself, rather than a mere category or group *in* itself.)

But if we know what the Third World is (or think we know), what about the first and second worlds? Both usages are in fact rare, and the latter almost nonexistent. Implicitly, the First World is the 'West', the Second World the 'East' – using West and East in a *political* sense, for capitalist and communist respectively.

However, as Worsley (1979) has pointed out, this poses a problem, since we now have both political (capitalist/communist) *and* economic (developed/underdeveloped) criteria at work. This should logically give us four categories, not three, because the Third World would then have to be divided into capitalist and communist Third World countries as well.

North/South. This is the most recent addition to the vocabulary of development, having been largely popularized by the Brandt Report (1980), in whose title it appears. Basically, 'North' = East plus West, and 'South' is the Third World. (It works quite well on a map, if you think about it; only Australia and New Zealand are awkward.)

But what is Development?

For the rest of this book I shall use all the above terms, blithely and more or less interchangeably. You should nonetheless now be aware of their somewhat differing resonances. However, there is a more sub-stantial issue to be addressed concerning 'development': namely what is it? Most of the literature tends to assume that the content of develop-ment is *economic*; i.e., usually, to increase national output and wealth, often by industrialization. But is this wholly valid? In principle, at least three other types of development goal can be distinguished.

(a) Social. When development studies got started as a field of study, after World War Two, it was taken for granted that the main problem was simply how to provide economic growth. Once this was done, it was assumed, the wealth thereby created would sooner or later 'trickle down' to the grass roots and make people better off – although this might not happen right away, Or, to put it another way, questions of *production* seemed much more important than arguments about *distribution*. As the late Kenyan politician Tom Mboya memorably put it, what is the use of arguing about how to cut the cake before you have even baked it?

This view was never universally accepted, however, and in recent years it has been widely criticized. An alternative view is to argue that, especially in the poorest countries, the prime task of development must be the immediate fulfilment of *basic needs*. These can be defined either broadly or narrowly. Minimally, they encompass food, shelter, and clothing; essential services, like drinking water, sanitation, health, education, transport; and job opportunities. Some would extend the concept to more qualitative factors: the environment, decision-making, and the rights of women and minorities.

For advocates of 'basic needs', merely maximizing growth of gross national product (GNP) is not development. More precisely, it neither *constitutes* development, nor will it necessarily *cause* development. At the same time, it would be misleading to suppose that you necessarily have to choose between *either* economic *or* social priorities in development. On the contrary, basic needs advocates would claim that theirs is a better *economic* strategy too: because a healthy, literate, and employed population is a better investment and an essential starting point for any development programme.

Still, it is interesting to note that attempts to create a social *indicator* (one that would measure social development, just as GNP per capita – arguably – measures economic development) reveal that countries may score very differently in each respect. A well-known social indicator is the Physical Quality of Life Index (PQLI): a weighted average of life expectancy, infant mortality, and adult literacy. Some countries with low per capita GNP, like Sri Lanka and Vietnam, score high on PQLI. (Thomas, 1983, p. 25ff.)

(b) Political. 'Political development' can often be a rather empty phrase, which ideologists of different persuasions then proceed to fill according to their own preconceptions. Thus American political scientists in the 1960s tended to use Western-style democracy as an index of political development; whereas by the 1970s some of them, ominously, had decided that maintaining 'order' even without democracy was more important. Others have claimed that the one-party systems found in many Third World as well as communist countries are either more appropriate or (even) more democratic.

A provocative attempt to redefine political, economic and social development was made in 1971 in a Tanzanian policy document called 'Mwongozo' (guidelines). This baldly stated:

> For people who have been slaves or have been oppressed, exploited, and disregarded by colonialism or capitalism, 'development' means 'liberation'. Any action that gives them more control of their own affairs is an action for development, even if it does not offer them better health or more bread. Any action that reduces their say in determining their own affairs or running their own lives is not development and retards them even if the action brings them a little better health and a little more bread. (cited in Rweyemamu et al, 1974, p. 24)

You can see the influence of dependency thinking here, in stressing autonomy and control over one's own destiny as political values, even at the expense of material development goals.

(c) **Cultural.** Almost inevitably, development involves cultural changes, often profound ones. The question is: what kind of changes? who says? and at what price? Probably the most striking example is in Iran; where the former Shah's modernisation strategy was evidently felt by many people to be profoundly un-Iranian, thus producing a specifically Islamic cultural reaction (rather than, as many had predicted, a Marxist political revolution) in the form of Ayatollah Khomeini. Iran today looks like a clear case in which the economic goals of development have been consciously subordinated to the cultural priority of creating a strictly Islamic society.

Nevertheless, as with political and social dimensions, I would argue that it is not usually a case of *either* cultural *or* economic development. Rather, if we look at examples of clear-cut economic development such as Japan, we find that tradition has not wholly been abandoned. Indeed, we can say that rapid and drastic modernization in some spheres may be accompanied and even *legitimated* by appeals to traditional values or practices in other spheres. The almost universal use of nationalism, by regimes of every kind, to mobilize their people for development is the most obvious case.

The Third World: a Descriptive Taxonomy

Generalizing about the Third World has its limitations. The societies which compose it are exceedingly diverse in all kinds of ways. Even in so short a book as this, it may be desirable to illustrate at least some of that diversity. This section will therefore give brief information about the major regions which make up the Third World.

1. Sub-Saharan Africa

Africa south of the Sahara has mostly tropical or subtropical climates. Physical environments range from rain forest to desert, with much savannah and bush land. Parts of Africa (e.g. South Africa, Zaire) are extremely rich in mineral resources. With localized exceptions, population density is low. Africa's major religions (as well as traditional animist beliefs) are Christianity and Islam; the latter has been established in West Africa for a thousand years and more, and continues to make gains.

Many pre-colonial African societies were relatively small-scale (sometimes called 'tribes', although controversy surrounds this word), and state formation had not proceeded far. There were major exceptions, though, e.g. the empires of Ghana and Mali in West Africa – names which were later taken by newly independent states.

Africa had a very specific experience of the world system and colonialism. First, it was uniquely subject to the massive depredations of the slave trade over some three centuries. Millions of people were forcibly taken to the Americas, with drastic effects on their societies. Secondly, formal colonialism in Africa was both late and comprehensive. It didn't really get going in earnest until after the Congress of Berlin in 1884–5, at which European powers carved up the map of Africa. But once it did get going it was almost universal: only Liberia and Ethiopia escaped.

The direct colonial phase lasted much less than a century. Most of Africa resumed its independence in the 1950s or 1960s. But the 50-odd states that have now come into existence are often small (in population), weak and fragmented; the ideology of 'Pan-Africanism' (calling for a united Africa) has had little concrete impact. Notoriously, the lack of fit between the new nations' boundaries and those of pre-colonial societies can lead to ethnic conflict being a major factor in political life.

Despite recent explosive urban growth, Africa remains overwhelmingly an agricultural continent. Much agricultural labour is done by women. The technological level is often low: the hoe (rather than bullock, let alone tractor) plus human muscle power remain the major instruments of production. All in all, in a Third World whose diversity is increasing, much of Africa looks to be the least developed and have the worst problems. For example, despite the predominance of agriculture many African states cannot feed themselves.

2. North Africa and West Asia (the 'Middle East')

This region stretches from Morocco to the Gulf, or perhaps beyond. It has a number of common characteristics. Much of it is desert, with long established agriculture along such major rivers as the Nile and Euphrates. 'Desertification' is quite a recent (and continuing) process in historical time; in Roman days, North Africa was the granary of the empire. The region is not rich in natural resources, with one crucial exception: oil.

This area was the cradle of the earliest known human civilizations, including of course Egypt. Much later, it was unified by the conquests of early Islam (which originated in what is now Saudi Arabia), and much of it thus acquired a common identity: a single written language, Arabic (although spoken variants can be mutually unintelligible); and a common faith, Islam (albeit with important sectarian differences, notably between Shias and Sunnis). Islamic seats of learning preserved the Graeco-Roman classics during Europe's 'dark ages', and also made important contributions to science.

Some places, Iran and Turkey, are Islamic but not Arab. Yet Turkey made its own contribution to the unity of the region in the form of the Ottoman Empire, which ended only with the First World War. Different coutries were also colonized or semi-colonized by France, Britain and Italy. In recent years, possession of the world's major oil resources has dramatically transformed both the wealth and importance of several states in this region.

3. South Asia

I use this term to designate what is sometimes called the 'Indian subcontinent'. It contains almost a billion people, most of whom live in one country, India. Historically it was the seat of a number of civiliz- ations, the last before the British Raj being the Moghuls. The Moghuls were Muslim, and Islam is the major religion of (and was indeed the basis for the creation of) Pakistan and Bangladesh. Hinduism is the main religion in India; its caste system has made it of special interest to sociologists. India is also the birth place of Buddhism, which is strong in Sri Lanka.

The area contains a relatively small number of rather large language- groups, and both India and Pakistan have experienced regional conflicts. Much of it, especially Bangladesh, is densely populated. Monsoon agriculture predominates. In some parts of India, notably the Punjab, the 'Green Revolution' has recently led to dramatic increases in yields, but in most of the region agrarian poverty remains widespread.

The unevenness of development within nations (and sectors), as well as between them, is illustrated by the little known fact that India is *also* the world's tenth ranking industrial power, and Indian transnational corporations (TNCs) are active elsewhere in the Third World.

4. East and South-East Asia

This region too is in a sense dominated by one country, China: with the world's largest population (around a billion), it is also the world's oldest continuously existing civilization, and its culture has long influenced the rest of the region. More recently, since the communist victory in 1949 it has been widely seen as a symbol (of hope or fear, depending on one's perspective) of an alternative socialist type of development; although trends since 1976 suggest that this may be changing.

Otherwise the area is rather diverse. The three other Chinese states – Taiwan, Hong Kong and Singapore – plus South Korea, form one category of small but dynamic capitalist industrializing countries. There are also six other Asian communist states around China, all but one hostile to it. Vietnam, Laos and Cambodia have not long emerged from decades of bloody war (or, in Cambodia, even bloodier aftermath under the genocidal Pol Pot regime); but North Korea and Mongolia have seen some industrialization. Meanwhile, Afghanistan seems likely to become the USSR's 'Vietnam'.

That leaves a number of diverse and sizeable countries. Their colonial experiences were varied: Thailand avoided it, Burma and Malaysia had the British, Indonesia (the world's fifth largest country by population, and immensely rich in natural resources) the Dutch, and the Philippines had Spain followed by the USA. (Indo-China was French). Religion is also very diverse: Buddhism is strong in several countries, Indonesia has Muslim and some Hindu influences, while Christianity has adherents in most places (including some 25% of the population of South Korea).

5. (a) Latin America

In some senses Latin America is the original Third World. It was colonized early, from the late fifteenth century, mostly by Spain and Portugal. It was also independent early, from as long ago as the 1820s (before most of Africa had even been colonized in the first place). The original inhabitants – still called Indians, for no better reason than that Columbus didn't know where he was – lived in societies which ranged from very small scale hunting and gathering bands to the major theocratic empires of the Inca, Aztec, and Maya. Their numbers today vary: almost non-existent in Argentina and Uruguay, a majority in Peru and Guatemala, but in no case possessing much power. Most were converted (often forcibly) to Christianity; but the traditional role of the Roman Catholic church in supporting an often oppressive status quo has in recent years been challenged from within, with the emergence of 'liberation theology'.

The continent's other inhabitants are descendants of voluntary settlers from Europe (and parts of Asia), and involuntary settlers from Africa. Population densities are mostly low. Many countries (especially Brazil) are rich in resources, which have been the basis for successive supplies to the West: gold and silver initially, then sugar, rubber, coffee, tin, copper, and much more.

In this century some larger countries – Brazil, Mexico, Argentina – have undergone a certain degree of industrialization, which continues. Whether this has or will transform the basic structures of under-development is hotly debated, and it is no surprise that it was Latin America that gave birth to dependency theory.

Politically, in the wake of Castro's triumph in Cuba most countries experienced guerilla movements, nearly all of which were crushed (including the death of Che Guevara in Bolivia in 1967). Political democracy has been precarious in most countries, with alternations of civilian and military regimes (the latter mostly, but not invariably, of the right). Today the smaller countries of Central America seem the focus of interest, with a recently victorious revolution in Nicaragua, and civil war in El Salvador.

(b) The Caribbean

This sub-region of the Americas perhaps deserves brief mention in its own right, having a number of sociologically distinctive features. Populated largely by the descendants of African slaves (and, in some cases, the Indian indentured labourers who followed them), it consists of a multiplicity of small, mostly island states. Historically dominated by plantation agriculture, Caribbean states find it hard for reasons of scale to diversify.

The region's languages are Spanish and French (Haiti) as well as English, reflecting a variety of colonizers who stayed a very long time (up to four centuries). The English-speaking territories, it is perhaps worth pointing out, are the one part of the Third World in which governments regularly lose office through the ballot box.

6. Conclusion

In the face of all the diversity, to dare to speak of a 'Third World' at all embodies a claim: that despite the endless variety of geography, history and culture, there is also at some level an element of commonality – in economy, politics, or society – in experience or structure. More precisely, there are at least two variants of this claim, corresponding to the two major perspectives in the field. To put this roughly, the two claims are:

a) **Recapitulation/Diffusion**. What the Third World shares is being 'behind' the advanced countries in various ways; it also shares the opportunity to ameliorate this by receiving benefits diffused from the West; and it will share a common future in following gradually in the West's footsteps.

b) **Unevenness/Dependence**. What the Third World shares is a similarity of experience; namely, being historically subjugated and reduced to a subordinate position in the world economy; which is not like anything the West went through; and which must be escaped from, not built upon, if real development is to take place.

Chapter Two
Theoretical Perspectives

Modernization versus Dependency Theory

I have already said that I shall use the above framework as a framework for this book – and this chapter in particular. The structure of this 'theory' chapter is as follows. I begin by comparing and contrasting one of the most famous examples of each school, W. W. Rostow and A. G. Frank. I go on to look at further varieties of modernization theory, and suggest tentatively that part of its agenda may still be valid. I also examine recent Marxist criticisms of dependency theory, especially by Warren. Finally, I mention Barrington Moore as an example of an important theorist who cannot be slotted readily into either of the two main camps.

Two Exemplars: Rostow and Frank

In order to illustrate the modernization and dependency perspectives, and the differences between them, we shall first look at the work of a major writer from each school. There are dangers in this procedure. Both these perspectives are in fact extremely diverse. Each contains within its boundaries different schools of thought, stressing different factors in development.

Also, by focussing on just two writers each of whom helped 'set up' the perspective in question, we run the risk of having a rather stale and dated analysis. Both Rostow and Frank produced their best-known work in the 1960s. But the world moves on, as does social science; new issues and debates have arisen, not least in response to these writers themselves.

Nonetheless, there is no denying that Rostow and Frank are both the best known and probably (for better or worse) the most widely influential representatives of the modernization and dependency paradigms, respectively. It is therefore appropriate to look at some of their major themes. In doing this, we shall also examine some of the criticisms and debate which their work has inspired and provoked.

Rostow

Walt Whitman Rostow is an American economic historian. Originally a specialist on British economic history, he became more widely famous (or even notorious) in two different spheres. As an academic, which most concerns us here, he coined and popularized the idea of a 'take-off' into self-sustaining economic growth as being the key stage of the development process; above all, in his book *The Stages of Economic Growth: a non-communist manifesto* (1960).

In addition, as that sub-title indicates, Rostow's work had political purpose. He explicitly (and rather immodestly) saw his theory of stages of economic growth as an alternative to Marx's. At the time of the Vietnam War he was an adviser to President Lyndon Johnson and acquired a reputation as a 'hawk': a role which helps to explain the sometimes bitter controversy which his work has evoked, especially from Marxists.

Rostow propounded a schema of five stages through which all developing societies must pass. The first of these he terms *traditional*. Although well aware that this lumps together a huge variety of actual societies, ranging from Stone Age cultures to (say) France on the eve of the Revolution, Rostow believes that for purposes of his model their common features matter more than the differences. These features include: 'pre-Newtonian' science and technology; a basically agricultural economy; and a rigidly ascriptive social structure, usually based in kinship.

In this sense, presumably, the vast majority of human societies – indeed, all of them until barely two hundred years ago – have been 'traditional'. In some, however, there began to be stirrings of new social forms and forces. This is Rostow's second stage, the *preconditions for take-off*. Often triggered off by some impulse from outside (although this is a point Rostow never systematically develops), changes begin across a whole range of institutions. In the economy, agriculture is augmented by an increase in trade, services, and the beginnings of industry (especially extractive industry, such as mining). The economy as a whole becomes less self-sufficient and localized, as trade and improved communications facilitate the growth of both national and international economies. Socially, these processes are related to the emergence of an elite group, able and willing to reinvest their wealth rather than squander it. Rational scientific ideas also play a key role: the natural world is no longer taken as given. At least one of the preconditions for social and economic progress is thus the *idea* that progress is possible at all, as opposed to fatalistic acceptance of the natural and social *status quo*.

This brings us to the key third stage, the *take-off* itself. Rostow characterises this in both quantitative and qualitative terms. Investment as a proportion of national income rises to at least 10%, thus ensuring that increases in per capita output outstrip population growth. One or more manufacturing sectors (but not, as yet, the whole range) come to assume a leading role. Political and social institutions more generally are reshaped in order to permit the pursuit of growth to take root. All this typically takes about twenty years, and Rostow attempts to date the actual take-off of those countries which have experienced them: 1783–1803 for Britain, which was the first; followed amongst others by the USA (1843–1860), Japan (1878–1900), Russia (1890–1914), and India and China (1950 onwards).

Rostow's last two stages can be dealt with briefly; in a sense, they are not part of the sociology of the Third World, inasmuch as any society that has got this far is by definition no longer underdeveloped. The *drive to maturity* is a period of consolidation. Modern science and technology are extended to most if not all branches of the economy, which thus acquires a wider range of leading sectors. The rate of investment remains high, at 10–20% of national income. Political reform continues, and the economy 'finds its feet' internationally.

Finally, there is the *age of high mass consumption*. This involves yet further consolidation and advance, and as such is not clearly distinct from the drive to maturity. Such is the productive power of the society by this stage that three broad strategic choices of orientation are available. Wealth can be concentrated in individual consumption, as in the USA; or channelled into a welfare state as in Western Europe; or used to build up global power and influence – which is how Rostow characterizes the USSR.

Such, in bare outline, is Rostow's theory. It has been extremely influential, perhaps especially at a common-sense level: the word 'take-off' has passed into ordinary use. It has also been hotly debated and fiercely criticized, from a variety of viewpoints. Before looking at some of the critique in detail, however, let us note some key characteristics of the *kind* of theoretical model that Rostow is using. Four linked aspects can be singled out: theoretical traits which Rostow arguably shares with others of the modernization school, even if his particular version is perhaps more extreme.

1. Rostow's theory is *evolutionist*. It sees socio-economic change as unfolding through a fixed set of stages.

2. It is also *unilinear*. All countries must pass by the same route, in the same order. There are no 'leaps', short cuts, choices, or alternative routes.

3. Further, it is *internalist*. Despite occasional tantalizing hints (as mentioned above) that outside influences do play a role, Rostow firmly takes the given society as his unit of analysis and assumes that all the crucial dimensions of change are internally generated within each society.

4. Finally, and in a sense summarising the above, it is *recapitulationist*. The presently underdeveloped countries today have to follow precisely the same basic path as did the now developed countries in their day. In this sense Rostow might even agree with Marx, who also said that the more developed society shows to the less developed the image of its own future.

How might such an account be criticized? A. G. Frank, in addition to putting forward a very different model of his own (see below), is the author of a major critique of the modernization approach in general and Rostow in particular. Frank (1969b) suggests three criteria for assessing any theory in the social sciences: empirical validity, theoretical adequacy, and policy effectiveness. (Crudely, we could thus ask: does it fit the facts? Does it make sense? and is it any use?)

Rostow has been found wanting on all three counts, and by no means solely by Marxists like Frank. Even to apply the model presents a host of difficulties, only some of which can be mentioned here. Thus other economic historians challenge on empirical grounds Rostow's central claim that an investment spurt characterizes the actual take-off. From a different tack, Frank himself points out that a number of countries in Latin America and elsewhere never had a 'traditional' stage at all, yet still seem to be locked into underdevelopment. He calls these *tabula rasa* (literally, 'clean state') countries; where there were either no pre-existing societies at all (e.g. Uruguay) or these were wiped out or marginalized by European conquest – which for Frank is where *both* the modern history of these countries *and* their underdevelopment begins.

The empirical problems in Rostow's work are linked to theoretical difficulties. There is wide agreement among critics that his major conceptual weakness consists in failing to emphasize *inter* – as well as *intra* – societal connections, i.e. relationships *between* as well as within societies. Thus for the Nobel prize winning Swedish economist, Gunnar Myrdal (1963) there are crucial differences in initial conditions faced by today's developing countries; not least, that they have to try to develop in a world context which *already* contains their precursors, i.e. a powerful block of already developed countries, whose interests may well clash with theirs (e.g. if they want to industrialize).

For other writers, the changed situation is in some ways actually beneficial. Thus the economic historian Alexander Gerschenkron (1962) has stressed what he calls the advantages of backwardness. On this view, late developing countries do *not* have to repeat the same stages as early developers; for example, they can use, where appropriate, technologies already developed elsewhere. But in either case the methodological point, and the critique of Rostow, are the same. Relations *between* countries, in space and time, are at least as important as what goes on within a society. In this sense, the evolving international context makes it likely – some would say certain – that stages or patterns of development are *not* everywhere the same. Reinhard Bendix has put this graphically: 'Industrialization cannot occur in the same way twice . . . Once [it] has occurred anywhere, this fact alone alters the international environment of all other countries' (quoted in Goldthorpe 1984, p. 137). Finally, over and above any empirical and theoretical weaknesses, Rostow's model is arguably not much help for policy purposes. For one thing, it seems as if the take-off can only be identified *ex post facto*, after the event (perhaps even decades after), which is not a lot of use to development planners in the here and now! Secondly, as Myrdal has acutely observed, there is in Rostow both a *teleology* and a problem of *agency*. That is to say, the process of take-off and growth is basically portrayed by Rostow as unfolding, in a rather automatic way, towards a given end-state; which makes it very difficult even to raise crucial questions of policy choice or planning development. Myrdal attributes this to Rostow's implicit bias in favour of laissez-faire capitalist development; which leads him to ignore the fact that virtually every single actual take-off (except perhaps those of the UK and the USA) has been an actively pursued project, in which the *state* has played a crucial economic role. This is as true of such capitalist take-offs as Bismarck's Germany or Meiji Japan as it obviously is of the USSR.

Frank

Andre Gunder Frank is an American economist – for all practical purposes; although he actually holds German citizenship – who received a conventional training in economics at Chicago. He went to

Latin America in the early 1960s, and drastically changed his views under the impact of both the Cuban Revolution and the then emerging 'dependency' school of thought. With the publication of his book *Capitalism and Underdevelopment in Latin America* (1969), followed by other works, Frank rapidly came to be taken in the English-speaking world as the leading representative of what has been variously called 'dependency', 'neo-Marxism', or 'underdevelopment theory'. In particular, his key term 'the development of underdevelopment' can be seen as the radical counterpart of Rostow's 'take-off'.

Whether methodologically or politically, Frank's starting point could scarcely be more different from Rostow's. Rather than taking a society as the unit of analysis, Frank sees national economies as structural elements in a global capitalist system. It is this system, not individual societies, which is the necessary unit of analysis.

Furthermore, this system is structured, and unevenly so. In a famous metaphor, Frank characterises it as a whole chain of 'metropolis-satellite' relations. This chain links the entire system: from the ultimate global metropolis which is no one's satellite (i.e. the USA); via a whole series of intermediate units which are simultaneously both metropolis and satellite (e.g. Latin American capital cities, which Frank sees as both exploited by the USA and themselves exploiting their own hinterlands); right down to the ultimate satellite – e.g. a landless rural labourer, who has nothing and no one to exploit (and, one should add these days, is probably female).

The nature of the whole chain is, to put it crudely, a gigantic and systematic rip-off. In Frank's terms, 'surplus' is continuously appropriated and expropriated upwards and outwards, at all levels, from bottom to top. This occurs because each metropolis has monopoly economic power in its bit of the system, rather than a free market. The system has been like this since it began (i.e. the 16th century, in Latin America), and remains so. Given this, any real development will require a revolutionary break from the system.

On the basis of this overall model, Frank formulates a number of more specific (although still pretty general) hypotheses. First, the development of satellites is limited simply because they are satellites. Development along metropolitan lines is precisely *not* possible for satellites, given their subordinate position in the system. What satellites experience is *under*development; which crucially Frank redefines as an active process of distortion, characteristic of the relatively modern fate of the Third World, and hence in no way to be equated with 'tradition' or any sort of original state. Conversely, the now developed countries never experienced *under*development, in this sense; they were only

*un*developed at the outset, which for Frank is very different.
In fact, Frank does not deny that some development has taken place
in Latin America. But his second hypothesis, consistent with his overall
approach, is that satellites can only develop when their ties with the
metropolis are relatively weakened. Frank offers two different sorts of
example of this. Isolation, whether geographical or economic – Frank
cites Paraguay at one time, and above all Japan – is not a bad but a
good thing, as it avoids satellization and permits 'self-generating'
development. Alternatively, once a country has become a satellite its
only chance is to seize brief opportunities when the grip of the
metropolis temporarily weakens – whether because of war or recession.
For example, for Frank such industrialization as a few Latin American
countries have achieved in this century was principally made possible
by the two World Wars and the 1930s depression.

This cannot last, however. Sooner or later the metropolis reasserts its
control, the errant satellite is reincorporated, and its briefly promising
development is 'choked off'. Exactly what processes this refers to is not
always clear, but Frank evidently has in mind the penetration of even
the more advanced Latin American economies in the 1960s by transnational corporations.

Frank's third hypothesis is perhaps the boldest of all. The regions
most 'ultra-underdeveloped' today, he asserts, are precisely those which
had the closest ties to the metropolis in the past. The Brazilian *nordeste*
(north-east) is probably his strongest case. Its appalling poverty and
apparent backwardness today are not in the least 'traditional', but on
the contrary in the days of 'King Sugar' this was originally the most
flourishing part of Brazil. It was, in a sense, used and then thrown on
the scrap-heap as economic interests 'moved on' both historically and
geographically.

As with Rostow, so with Frank. Utterly opposed as their perspectives
are, we shall follow the same procedure of first drawing out some
characteristics of Frank's theoretical model as such, before passing on
to some specific criticisms.

1. Frank's model is *externalist*. At least for the Third World, all
decisive and determining change is seen as coming from, and imposed
by, outside forces.

2. It is also *bilinear*. Metropolis and satellites pursue totally different
paths from the beginning, determined by their different structural roles
in the system.

3. Further, it is *stagnationist*. For the satellite, and in some sense for
the system as a whole, nothing ever changes: the structure remains the
same. (This may sound rather absurd: evidently Frank is not claiming

that the world or any part of it is exactly the same today as it was four centuries ago. Nonetheless, his concept of 'continuity-in-change' definitely emphasises the continuity rather than the change.)

4. Finally, it is *discontinuist*. So far from following in the footsteps of metropolitan development, the satellite not only starts out on a different road (albeit a road not of its own choice, and one which turns out to be a cul-de-sac), but will have to make a radical break with the entire system if it ever wants to really develop. In no sense does development emerge by evolution within the system. Frank never specifies what this involves, but at least initially he seems to have taken Cuba as an example.

Passing now to more specific criticisms, one could say that Frank's own aforementioned three criteria for assessing theories have boomeranged back on him. Certainly critics have identified empirical, theoretical, and policy weaknesses in his work as they have with Rostow. Empirically, indeed, the criticisms are very similar. It turns out to be often difficult to apply Frank's model – in particular, his view that no real development at all is possible under capitalism. It is far from clear what this means; but if it means what it appears to mean then it appears not to be true. For, while some aspects of North-South relations past and present seem to fit Frank's model, others equally clearly do not, e.g. the growth of 'newly industrialising countries'.

Secondly, with Frank as with Rostow, critics have attributed empirical problems to theoretical deficiencies. It is difficult to identify his 'metropolis' and 'satellite' with any actual sociological entity: they are a curious mix of geographical and social, being apparently constituted at different levels by countries, classes, or even individuals.

Finally, there are policy problems. Even supposing Frank's analysis to be correct, what is to be done? Presumably, one must 'delink' from the world system in some way. Yet it is not clear in what sense this is possible. Frank himself, like Wallerstein, now seems to regard even communist countries which have tried to go it alone (like Cuba) as being still bound up in the world system. Here too, perhaps, less sweeping and polarized alternatives would seem more apt, looking in detail at practical and feasible ways of trying to reduce dependence without hoping to abolish it entirely.

Critics of Dependency Theory

Naturally, dependency theory had always been liable to counterattack and critique from the 'right', by modernization approaches. More unexpected, perhaps, was an increasingly vigorous assault from the 'left' which gathered momentum in the late 1970s and early 1980s, by critics for whom dependency theory in various ways was not Marxist *enough*. The best known of the these critics is Bill Warren.

Warren

Despite the recent dominance of dependency theory, being an avowed Marxist is not inconsistent with enthusiastic support for capitalism as a means of promoting development. Thus the late Bill Warren, in his book *Imperialism: Pioneer of Capitalism* (1980), argued vigorously and heretically that:

(a) The prospects for capitalist development in much of the Third World are good;

(b) Such development has in fact already been taking place – i.e. in the spread of both capitalist relations and the development of the productive forces, in both industry and agriculture – especially in the period since 1945;

(c) Even before that, 'colonialism itself acted as a powerful engine of progressive social change': not only in destroying pre-existing social systems, but also in implanting a capitalism which has now taken firm root;

(d) *Internal* aspects of the Third World (e.g. traditional institutions and ideas) are more of an obstacle to development than is 'imperialism';

(e) The net effect of the relationship between 'imperialist' and Third World countries is beneficial to the latter's economic development and even industrialisation;

(f) The rise of 'indigenous' capitalisms' in various places means that we are now living in 'an era of declining imperialism and advancing capitalism';

(g) Although this theme is very 'underdeveloped' in Warren's work, he believes, as a Marxist, that the above trends will lead to the creation of an industrial proletariat and ultimately to socialism;

(h) The *nationalism* prevalent in much of the Third World is for Warren wholly negative: it puts a brake on capitalist development and it diverts the proletariat away from pure socialism.

In making such claims, Warren was self-consciously breaking with not only dependency theory, but *also* the whole Marxist traditional view of imperialism as harmful to the Third World – although Warren claimed his own view was closer to Marx's own.

Not surprisingly, Warren's views have provoked a storm of criticism.

(i) Although some countries may be developing or even industrializing, this does not prove that all others can or will follow. The argument here is similar to one in social mobility studies: the fact that some individuals rise out of one class into another does not mean that classes themselves thereby cease to exist. On the contrary, by relieving potential tension such mobility may actually strengthen the class system, not weaken it.

(ii) Warren's rosy view of colonialism (he never mentions the slave trade!) and stress on internal Third World obstacles are viewed by some as both inaccurate and insulting: a form of 'blaming the victim', and theoretically a step backwards into what is in effect a version of the crude tradition/modernity division associated with modernization theory.

(iii) More subtly, his obsessional hatred of nationalism seems unrealistic as well as inconsistent, since by his own account it is national independence which has led to today's greater freedom of manoeuvre for the Third World to develop.

Although Warren's is an unusually extreme view, aspects of his critique of dependency theory are shared by others, both Marxist and non-Marxist. In a sense, the extreme formulations of some versions of dependency theory (e.g. A. G. Frank) have produced an equally extreme counterblast. In the mid 1980s, a somewhat more moderate dependency position might well concede some points, while standing firm on others. Thus:

1. Historically, the 'creation of the world' *was* a drastic, contra-dictory, often brutal process, creating global inequalities which persist to this day.

2. Some countries may still industrialise, but the overall system remains structurally unequal.

3. Capitalist development is a dynamic but profoundly uneven process, benefitting some and disadvantaging others at many levels: individual, class, nation, and gender.

4. Rather than falsely polarizing 'external' versus 'internal' obstacles to development we must focus on how they are *linked* (e.g. alliances between TNCs and local Third World bourgeoisies).

5. To speak of a Third World is simply to recognize that for some groups in particular contexts – most of the world's population, in fact – the economic and social structures they face differ strikingly in degree, and probably in kind as well, from those in the already industrialised capitalist countries.

6. But generalization is unwise. If it was wrong to deny with Frank that capitalism could any longer develop the Third World, it would be equally misguided to assume with Warren that a *general* process of

capitalist development is now unfolding. Each concrete case must be examined on its merits.

Varieties of Modernization Theory

There's obviously much more to modernization theory than Rostow alone. The feature he most clearly illustrates is a *stages* approach. What other theoretical 'moves' are typical of modernization theory?

One very common tendency, going back to the sociological classics, is to picture development not so much as a series of stages but as a basic *dichotomy*, or pair of opposites. You're probably familiar already with Tonnies 'gemeinschaft/gesellschaft' (community/association), or Durkheim's 'mechanical vs organic solidarity'. In modern times, Talcott Parsons' 'pattern variables' have been used by Hoselitz (1960) in a similar way. All you do, basically, is set up two opposite pairs of characteristics, and then claim that one lot are 'traditional' and apply to the Third World, while the other lot are 'modern' and apply to the West. So, for example, the West is described as achievement-orientated and having a highly specialized division of labour, while the Third World is the opposite: ascriptive oriented (it's not what you achieve, but who you're born, that counts), and with very little role specialization.

One problem with this kind of 'study of paired contrasts' is that there's no movement in it, no process. This can be remedied by a second approach, *diffusionism*. On this view, development consists of those who've got it giving it (or some of it) to those who haven't. Depending on the author, the 'it' can be anything from capital or technology to political institutions or cultural values. This is the theoretical basis for the idea of *aid*. On this view, too, even *within* a Third World country the same process takes place. There is a 'traditional' sector and a 'modern' sector, and development means that the modern will gradually spread its influence and absorb the traditional. Such theories (of which there are several kinds, economic and sociological) are known – for obvious reasons – as *dualist*.

A third approach in modernization theory might be called *psychologism*. It's tempting to call this one 'When All Else Fails', since so often that seems to have been the mood in which it has been taken up. Despairing of finding economic or social or political explanations for underdevelopment, this approach locates the problem firmly in the *cultures* (or even the psyches) of Third World peoples – who are thus said to be passive, conservative, fatalistic, or superstitious, when what they need is to be creative, innovative, entrepreneurial, get-up-and-go types.

What can we say about these different 'modernization' approaches (which I've only sketched here)? For one thing, they're rather too close for comfort to Western 'commonsense' ideas about development. You should remind yourself what the alternatives are. A dependency theorist like Frank would reject dichotomies, firstly, saying we have long lived in a single, capitalist world: *nothing* is 'traditional' any more, even if it looks that way. Likewise, Frank would reject *diffusionism*, or at least re-evaluate it. In his (perhaps extreme) view, the West has 'diffused' nothing but trouble to the Third World: political oppression, economic exploitation, and the very structures of under-development itself. As for *psychologism*, Frank would see this as 'blaming the victim', and as such implicitly racist.

Others (including other Marxists) may take a more balanced view. Perhaps some traditional sectors do survive, even if linked to capitalism. Probably the balance sheet of 'diffusion' isn't either wholly positive or wholly negative: there has been good and bad. As for 'psychologism', while avoiding extremes we can surely recognize – in the spirit of Weber's famous 'Protestant Ethic' – that there do exist real sociological questions about socio-cultural innovation: who does it, when, where, and why? Yet, like Weber (but unlike psychological approaches to development) we should avoid monocausal determinism, i.e. singling out one factor alone as *the* key to the whole process. Instead, we need to look at the interplay of economic *and* cultural and other factors, in concrete cases. There is, I would argue, too little work on cultural aspects in the sociology of development. Dependency theory has become *over*-economistic. Maybe to pay *some* attention to culture could be a lesson which modernization theory still has to teach us.

Barrington Moore's 'Routes'

By no means all contributions to the sociology of development can be easily pigeon-holed as 'modernization' or 'dependency'. An outstanding example is the influential work of Barrington Moore (1966), which might be described as modernization in form and Marxist (but not dependency, as we shall see) in content.

Moore looks at what he calls the 'routes to the modern world' followed in six countries: Britain, France, the USA, Japan, China, and India. He is particularly concerned to explore connections between the types of political regime which resulted from modernization, and the varying patterns of class alliances which preceded and precipitated it.

Importantly for Moore, these classes include losers as well as winners; and his overall focus is less on the characteristic inheritors and protagonists of industrial society, the bourgeoisie and proletariat, than on their agrarian counterparts – the 'lord and peasant' of his book's subtitle. Particularly crucial is how these classes respond to the challenge of commercial agriculture.

On the basis of his six case studies (and making reference also to Germany and Russia), Moore delineates three 'routes to the modern world'. The first – as in Britain, France, and the USA – is *bourgeois revolution* leading to *capitalist democracy*. Here a social group develops with an independent economic base, namely an urban trading and/or manufacturing class, and attacks obstacles to its economic and political success. Its allies in this process vary markedly. The old landed upper class either form part of the tide, as in England; or if hostile are swept away by revolution (as in France) or civil war (as in the USA, where the Southern plantocracy rather awkwardly fill this slot). As for peasants, they either pushed the same way (France), or were overwhelmed by the capitalist advance (England, e.g. the enclosures), or they never existed in the first place (USA).

Route two is variously characterized as *revolution from above*, 'capitalist and reactionary', or 'abortive revolution'. Its eventual outcome, at least temporarily, is *fascism*. In Germany and Japan (and presumably Italy), the bourgeois impulse is much feebler, and any attempted bourgeois revolution crushed. Instead, a relatively weak commercial-industrial class relies on dissident elements (junkers, samurai) from the older and still dominant ruling class to force through a programme of economic modernization from above. This can lead to rapid industrialization, but within strict political limits.

In route three, finally, the dead weight of the great agrarian bureaucracies of Russia and China stifled even more effectively any impulses to commercial or industrial (let alone political) modernization, whether from below or above. Since the new urban classes were too weak – and the old classes, in a sense, too stupid – there remained in the absence of modernization a huge peasantry, which would ultimately overthrow the old order. So route three is *peasant revolution* and its outcome *communism* – which then proceeds, as Moore lugubriously notes, to make those same peasants its victims.

And India? A check on generalization, it seems, since it cannot (at least as yet) be readily slotted into any category. Its particular history means that no class has been constituted in such a way as to have an interest in rechanneling agricultural surplus so as to get growth started. Aspects of democracy coexist alongside much rural misery, yet there is little sign of revolution. India, one senses, represents unfinished business.

Moore's work has been massively influential, or at least inspirational. His development of Marxist class categories in a comparative framework firmly grounded in empirical evidence has proved something of a model for more recent large-scale comparative grand theorizing, such as the work of Perry Anderson, Theda Skocpol, and Immanuel Wallerstein. He graphically showed that development was not a smooth process, but one full of conflicts and revolutions. (Even his chapter on England is titled 'England and the contribution of violence to gradualism'.) And Moore showed both the importance and the specificity of history. In all this, his work represented an implicit blow against culturalist, unilinear, or evolutionist strands in modernization theory.

On the other hand, it has proved persistently difficult to apply Moore's perspectives more widely. Moore himself cautioned against this, insisting that what he said only applies to the countries he said it about. In particular, he chose not to study 'small' countries on the grounds that 'the decisive causes of their politics lie outside their own boundaries' (1966, p. xiii). This indicates the major respect in which Moore remains closer to modernization than to dependency theory. In his study just about everything – even for India, which was after all a colony – is explained by events or trends inside the society concerned.

This leads Moore to ignore the crucial question which a dependency theorist might ask, namely: how far is the 'availability' of a particular route to any country at a given time determined by the routes which other countries have already followed. It hardly seems coincidental that Moore's three routes and six cases also form a *chronological* sequence. In a nutshell, might not the earlier success of the UK *et al.* have made it harder for 'latecomers' to follow the same road, and hence made more statist and/or revolutionary approaches more likely?

Chapter Three
Industrialization

Introduction

Industrialization is at once a central and an elusive topic in the sociology of development, as indeed in sociology more generally. Its centrality lies in the fact that it is the advent of modern industry, above all else, which is widely held to clearly distinguish contemporary Western society as a whole from all previous social forms. In this sense, the Industrial Revolution is cited by Nisbet (1967) as one of the 'two revolutions' – the other being political, namely, the French Revolution – whose transforming impact gave rise amongst other things to the new discipline of sociology itself. In similar vein, Lee and Newby (1983) have recently used various aspects of industry and industrialization as a peg on which to hang an entire introductory textbook in sociology.

These examples also illustrate the topic's elusiveness, in the sense that in such approaches there is little to prevent 'industrialization' from becoming equated with the entire subject matter of sociology. Similarly, there has been much debate as to whether we should still characterize Western societies as 'industrial', or prefer some other term such as 'post-industrial' (see for instance Kumar, 1978). Likewise, those interested in East/West comparisons have argued over whether there is a 'logic of industrialism', such that the political differences between the USA and USSR will gradually be eroded in a process of 'convergence' (Kerr, 1962).

These are interesting and important issues, but I shall not deal with them here. My focus will be narrower, in two senses. First, although not denying that the growth of industry links in to broader processes of social change (e.g. urbanization), I have tried to cover at least some of those processes in other chapters and will not repeat them here.

Secondly, this chapter will specifically address what might be called the 'North-South' issue in industrialization, namely: can the same or similar processes of industrialization as characterized the West's own development be expected to recur in the Third World? Are they indeed already taking place? Can we look forward eventually to a wholly industrialized world? Or are there reasons why this is impossible, unlikely, or even undesirable?

Definitions

A particularly clear and helpful account of many of the issues covered in this chapter has recently been provided by Wield (1983). In terms of definitions of industry, Wield suggests three. One is *residual*: 'industry' means everything that isn't agriculture. Another is *sectoral*: energy, mining and manufacturing. More useful than either of these, however, is the third: 'a particular way of organizing production using machinery and a complex division of labour'.

This last definition is better because it is more discriminating than the other two. No. 1, for instance, wouldn't allow us to speak of industrialized agriculture; while no. 2 fails to distinguish *scale* of production – often very varied in the Third World. Plumping for no. 3, then, Wield suggests this can be unpacked in either of two ways, which we might call 'micro' and 'macro' respectively: the industrial production as such, and the broader social process of industrialization. Although as already stated our main concern is with the latter, it is important to have a fairly precise idea of the former too, and I cannot do better than quote Wield's definition (adding my own emphases):

'Industrial production processes are characterized by:
(a) the possibility of utilizing *technologies* with complex *machinery* associated with a large *scale* of production;
(b) the utilization of a wide range of *raw materials* often already processed through the use of complex technologies;
(c) a relatively complex *technical division of labour* within units of production;
(d) complex *co-operation and co-ordination* of specialized tasks inside the unit of production;
(e) a diverse range of *skills* within the work force.' (Wield, 1983, p. 8.)

As Wield observes, the distinctiveness of all this becomes clearer if we contrast all the above with small-scale *artisan* or intermediate *handicrafts* production. It is characteristic of the Third World that all these co-exist side by side. This leads into the second, broader or 'macro' notion of industrialization. Briefly put, this implies that the 'micro' model outlined above will spread, and carry all before it sooner or later, with consequent broad social changes. Whether this is indeed on the cards in the Third World is precisely the issue of this chapter. That it cannot be taken for granted is already clear from the case of *extractive* industry (mining), long prevalent since colonial times in parts of the Third World without necessarily having any 'spill-over' transformative effects on the wider society as a whole.

In order to capture these broader aspects, a single measure is not enough. Sutcliffe (1971), the author of a major study on industry and underdevelopment, proposed a threefold definition of an industrialized country as one where the industrial sector: (i) contributes at least 25% of GDP (gross domestic product); (ii) consists 60% or more of manufacturing; and (iii) employs more than 10% of the population. We shall see how Sutcliffe applies this below.

Strategies for Industrialization

Looking at the specifically economic choices faced and paths pursued by Third World governments today and in the recent past, we can distinguish two broad types of development strategy; corresponding at least roughly to the modernization/dependency dichotomy. First, however, we should recall that the traditional economic role for the Third World was not industrial at all, but rather to specialize in producing minerals or cash crops to 'feed' the industrialization of the West. Despite the changes discussed below, this model still characterizes the economic structures of many Third World countries (above all, in Africa). It is also still legitimated by a powerful strand of conventional neo-classical economic wisdom. The doctrine of *comparative advantage* (from Ricardo onwards) advocates that countries should specialize in those branches of production in which they have 'natural' advantages. On this argument, raw material production is what Third World countries are good at and suited for, at present. By specializing in this area, and exchanging their raw materials for industrial goods produced elsewhere, they will eventually earn enough revenue to permit local capital accumulation and hence a gradual diversification of their economic structures.

This model has been much criticized. Empirically, there is a persisting (and probably insoluble) debate about the *terms of trade* between raw materials and industrial goods. Some economists, like Gunnar Myrdal (1963), believe that the long-run trend is against raw material producers; that is (over-simplifying somewhat), the more you produce, the less (relatively) you earn. On this view, then, putting all your eggs in the basket of primary production is a dead end, because you will never in fact earn enough to make the switch to industrialization. Instead, like Lewis Carroll's Red Queen, it takes all the running you can do even to stay in the same place; because year by year the price you must pay to import industrial goods consumes an ever greater proportion of your own earnings from primary products. Whether or not this is universal or inevitable, it certainly corresponds to the actual experience of a number of Third World countries.

1. Import-substituting Industrialization (ISI). The critique summarized above was first formulated by an important group of Latin American economists from the 1940s onwards. Including the Argentinian Raul Prebisch and the Brazilian Celso Furtado, this group is known as ECLA (after the UN Economic Commission for Latin America, where many of them worked). Sometimes their approach is also called 'structuralist', which in a sociological context can be rather confusing.

Rather than *development towards the outside* (as above), the ECLA group advocated *development towards the inside*. In practice – and, since several of them went on to hold government office, this *was* a practice and not just a theory – this took the form of *import-substituting industrialization* (ISI). The idea here was that, rather than specializing in primary production for export, you should try to cut down on imports of industrial goods by manufacturing at least some of them locally. This did not mean basic or heavy industrialization (steelworks, etc.), at least not at first; but more likely light industries producing consumer goods (textiles, household products, soft drinks, etc.) for the home market. Because value-added is greater in industry than agriculture or mining, this would be a surer way of accumulating capital and later diversifying the economy.

As is often the case, this was not a purely economic doctrine. The ECLA group had a political and social project too. Representing in a sense the outlook of a new but weak industrial middle class, they wanted to modernize and overhaul what they regarded as the backward and even feudal social structures of their countries. In particular, they hoped to erode the power of the coalition of traditional rural landlords and import-export merchants who effectively ruled in much of Latin America. Further, they wished to enfranchise (often literally) the working classes and peasants, thus creating a modern democratic political community and an integrated national society. All in all, this was a programme with strong echoes of the French Revolution and the world-view of a rising bourgeoisie.

As a practical strategy, however, it ran into difficulties. One area of controversy focusses on the role of the state. Although not socialist, the ECLA approach was not content to leave everything to market forces; regarding them not as natural, but as the outcome of an unequal specialization which had been imposed upon Latin America historically by the Spanish and Portuguese colonialists. So they saw an economic role for the state, in particular to create tariff barriers to shelter the new infant industries during their early years.

Neo-classical critics, however, said this was inefficient. In the absence of competition, there was no way of choosing rationally what branches of production you should specialize in. Also, protected markets have a habit of remaining so well beyond infancy, leading to a maze of tariff barriers which serve no function except to inhibit trade and growth. Although there is a strong dose of ideology in these arguments, it is probably true that in many cases tariffs were applied with insufficient finesse.

A second problem with ISI was that it produced a peculiar kind of vicious circle. To set up industries, you obviously need capital goods. In the first instance, these must be imported; which means they must be paid for, with foreign exchange. How to earn the foreign exchange? In the short run, what option was there but to concentrate even more intensively on the traditional primary production for export; which of course is what you're trying to get away from, but right now it's all you've got!

There was an alternative source of funds, but that had its problems also. The ECLA approach originally had nothing against foreign capital as such, so in many cases the answer was to invite foreign companies in to do the industrializing. But this too often backfired. In theory, foreign capital was supposed to help set up branches of industry and thereby stimulate local business to follow suit. In practice, TNCs (transnational corporations) increasingly came to monopolize these new markets into which they had been invited. Not only did they not encourage local firms, but often they actually displaced or swallowed them up. After all, it is not easy for a small new indigenous enterprise to compete against the resources, know-how, assets, and sheer power of a TNC. So, paradoxically, the ISI strategy which had been intended to create less dependent and more autonomous economies all too often ended up trapped in new forms of dependence.

Even if these problems could have been overcome, there was a third source of difficulty with ISI. It assumed the existing pattern of demand.

If your industrialization consists of making at home what you currently import, then what are these goods? In practice, given the highly unequal income distribution in countries where most people lack effective purchasing power, this means concentrating on the luxury goods consumed by a small elite: televisions, consumer durables, cars, etc. An industrial strategy based on those sorts of goods simply reproduced the existing inequalities: it had no relevance to basic needs, and it did nothing to put purchasing power in the hands of the mass of the people and unleash the kind of Keynesian dynamic of large-scale demand which the ECLA group had intended. It was a skewed, wrong-way-round sort of industrialization: starting with what in Europe's industrialization had come later, and only then (if ever) going on to the sort of basic industrialization and mass consumption goods which Europe had begun with.

2. **Export-oriented Industrialization (EOI).** The crisis and blockage of ISI lent weight to a very different approach which increasingly emerged in the late 1960s and 1970s, especially in parts of Latin America and East Asia. (The contrast between Brazil before and after the 1964 military coup is probably the most striking example.) In one sense the strategy of *export-led* growth was not novel; in that it advocated production for the world market rather than for home demand as an engine of growth, and it justified this in terms of the doctrine of comparative advantage.

Two things were new, however. The obvious one is the *content* of the exports: no longer the traditional agriculutral and mineral primary products, these now comprised manufactured goods. In the first instance, these were and to a large extent still are light industrial products, especially textiles. (Check where your own clothes and shoes were made, and you'll see what I mean!) Increasingly, however, several *newly industrializing countries* (NICs) have diversified into such areas as electronics, steel, ship-building, and even computers.

The second novelty is more contentious. Although the NICs profess an often brashly capitalist ideology, closer inspection reveals that their growth has by no means been the work of market forces unaided. On the contrary, their economies are characterized by often massive *state intervention* – not infrequently on as large a scale as was ever the case with ISI! From Brazil to Taiwan, Mexico to South Korea, these are highly statist economies (Wade and White, 1984).

Needless to say, the NICs have not been without their critics. Dependency theory in particular obviously finds them a great challenge (it shouldn't be happening!), and has tried to develop a critique; some parts of which are more convincing than others. For example, it stretches credulity to argue that the NICs represent 'development of underdevelopment', in A. G. Frank's sense. On whatever index you choose – quantitative growth rates, structural change (e.g. from agriculture to industry, or from light to heavy industry), and in many cases actual incomes and living standards – there has been undeniable progress. Indeed, I think one has to admit that what has been called the 'stagnationist' thesis of dependency theory – i.e. Frank's extreme view, that no further progress under capitalism is possible anywhere in the Third World – has been definitely disproved by the experience of the NICs.

However, to concede this does not exhaust the dependency critique. There are at least three more strings to the dependency bow, and these may be more on target. One is to suggest that all this has been accomplished under the dominance of foreign capital, hence it does not constitute genuine or autonomous development. I'll return to this.

A different tack is to point to the *political preconditions* of this economic model. The NICs' comparative advantage is based on low wages, kept low by political suppression of trades unions and democracy. It is true that virtually all NIC governments are more or less politically authoritarian. It is not clear, however, at least to me, that they are more authoritarian than most other Third World governments, of left or right; the great majority of which have not 'delivered the goods' economically speaking, as the NICs have. (This is not to condone authoritarian government anywhere, but merely to make a comparative sociological observation.)

To further confuse the picture, the conventional economists' measure of inequality – the Gini coefficient – appears to suggest that at any rate the East Asian NICs (notably Taiwan and South Korea) have rather *less* inequality than most other Third World countries. Likewise on low wages, it would seem that most NICs have now moved on from what was undoubtedly their original selling point of cheap labour, into industries which are more skill and capital-intensive. This can be seen most clearly in textiles, which are increasingly shifting to countries like Indonesia, Morocco, or even China – where wages are appreciably lower than in NICs like South Korea.

This last consideration leads conveniently into dependency theory's strongest argument against the NICs. Rather than a rearguard action which says it isn't happening, or that anyway it isn't development, this focusses wisely on the *generalizability* of the NICs' experience as a *model*. If they can do it, does that mean everybody can and should do it? Certainly, in the ideological struggles which are rarely far below the surface in scholarly economic debates, this is what is usually claimed. The NICs are frequently touted as sensible, practical regimes, which have followed the natural laws of economics instead of trying to impose alien or unworkable ideologies, and hence have reaped a rich reward.

And this message is widely believed. Thus many other Third World countries have been busily setting up *export processing zones* (EPZs): enclaves into which foreign investors are invited, on very generous terms (infrastructure provided, import duties waived, tax holidays, full remission of profits, etc.), to employ cheap local labour (often female) producing light industrial goods for export. They hope thereby to repeat the experience and success of the NICs. But will they? It is perhaps too early to tell, but even so there are strong reasons for doubt.

Clearly the argument hinges on what you think have been the conditions for and causes of the NICs' success, and whether these conditions exist or could be replicated in other parts of the Third World. One problem is that there is no general agreement on what the key factors are, so the discussion that follows can only be suggestive, at best. One *internal/cultural* consideration would be to note that the East Asian NICs, the so-called 'four little tigers' or 'gang of four' – Taiwan, Singapore, Hong Kong and South Korea – have a common link: three are wholly or overwhelmingly Chinese, and the fourth shares with them a strongly Confucian cultural heritage. On this basis, by a kind of analogy with Weber's 'Protestant Ethic', there has been suggested a 'Confucian ethic' for these countries, emphasizing such values as respect for authority, social cohesion, and education as a basis for their economic success.

I doubt that this is the whole story, and obviously it doesn't explain Brazil; but equally, I doubt that such factors can be wholly ruled out. In which case, other countries which lack Confucianism or a similarly strong fundamental ethic presumably will not be able to follow suit on this basis. (As a caution against single-factor explanations, however, you should notice that another thing which the 'gang of four' (partially excepting Singapore) have in common is that they are almost wholly *mono-ethnic*, a very unusual situation in the Third World; hence the ethnic and national problems which stymie so many other countries' progress simply don't arise, which is an obvious bonus.)

Most dependency critiques, however, emphasize *external/economic* factors. They point out that the NICs 'took off' in the 1960s, at a time when the world (and in particular the Western) economy was still growing, and did so by specializing in labour-intensive areas such as textiles which the increasingly capital-intensive and high-wage Western economies either could afford to shed and lose or simply could not compete in. Several things, arguably, have changed since then. One is that the existing NICs have (so to speak) taken up all the space there is, often literally, as Western countries turn increasingly protectionist and put up tariff barriers and quotas against textiles and electronic goods produced in Third World countries, in order to protect their own troubled industries in these fields. This growing protectionism in turn is a product of the deep recession which has gripped the world economy for over a decade, and which shows no clear sign of easing yet. So who are all the new would-be NICs going to sell the products of their EPZs to?

Some might say this is an unduly static or short-sighted view. It is true that dependency theorists have often held to a *zero-sum* view of world capitalism, assuming that a gain in one part of the system automatically entails a loss somewhere else. As such, they tend to overstress how much capitalist development has been achieved *externally* (some places exploiting other places), and underestimate how much is due to *internal* factors (increases in productivity brought about by technical progress). More generally, Marxists of all kinds are all too prone to wishful thinking, pronouncing capitalism to be dead or moribund – when time and again it proceeds to confound them by making a miraculous recovery.

Yet even allowing for all that, I would still stick my neck out and suggest that for many countries EPZs and export-led growth will turn out to be a cruel con-trick, and no less a dead-end than was the traditional export of primary products. The world (read 'Western') market is limited, and currently stagnant and saturated. Most countries setting up EPZs have little to offer except cheap labour (indeed, they must compete with each other to see who can be the cheapest – a contest in which the all-time winner now seems likely to be China, of all places!). This may enable them to get a slice of labour-intensive industries like textiles, but it is hard to see how they will make the crucial shift which the NICs have made into either traditional heavy or more technically advanced industries.

Above all, and quite unlike the NICs of East Asia or Latin America, most EPZ-mongers seem content to pin all their hopes on foreign businesses. Rather than encouraging either state enterprise or indigenous firms, they are left at the mercy of TNCs who as a result have a field day. Thanks to recent advances in technology and communications, TNCs are thus enabled to do two very convenient things.

1) They can *break down* their production processes into discrete components and physically locate each one where it can be done most

cheaply. This means that Third World countries do not acquire entire industries, but only those stages which are labour intensive – and hence most technologically backward. This *decomposition* of production processes has gone further than many people realize. In the semi-conductor industry which underpins the current revolution in electronics and computers, it is quite usual for the components to be manufactured in an advanced country, assembled in a Third World country (this is the labour-intensive stage: e.g. 'sewing' silicon chips together, a task largely performed by young women workers in South East Asia, often recruited explicitly under racist and sexist slogans about 'the traditional nimble fingers of the oriental female'); and then returned to the advanced country for final processing and packaging. Another example is of trousers, cut out in West Germany, airfreighted across the Mediterranean to Tunisia to be made up, then flown back to Germany for finishing and sale. Quite likely, your own jeans or calculator or stereo have been produced on this roundabout basis.

2) Even without this decomposition, the *competition* between different Third World countries to attract customers to their own EPZs is a virtual incitement to TNCs to play off one against another. You set up in one place, take advantage of all the grants and tax concessions, and then when these are finished you just pull out, set up somewhere else, and take another set of hand-outs. Nor is this process confined to Third World countries. If you live anywhere north of Watford, you may well be aware of examples in your own region. With both national and local governments, in the West as well as in the Third World, increasingly desperate to attract new jobs to their own communities, it is hard to see how this situation will quickly change. Needless to say, the ever-present threat of potential relocation also acts as a powerful curb on trade union campaigns for better wages or conditions.

I have deliberately spent some time on this discussion of NICs, EPZs, TNCs and so forth, because these are the key development issues of the 1980s and 1990s. In many ways they strain and take us beyond the 'modernization vs dependency' framework, which I have largely used to structure this book and which served us well enough in the 1960s and 1970s. Even so, I shall conclude this section by suggesting that at least one version of dependency theory can cope with the NICs. This is Wallerstein's *world-system theory*.

Whereas A. G. Frank uses a dichotomous model of *metropolis* and *satellite* to characterize the world system, Wallerstein makes a triple distinction: *core, periphery* and *semi-periphery*. This addition of a third term makes the model much more plausible and flexible. Instead of being committed to maintaining the 'development of underdevelopment', Wallerstein can thus predict that *sometimes* (not always) *some* countries (not all) can move up or down. More precisely, at times of economic recession in the existing core he predicts that there is limited scope for a few countries to rise in the system, either by 'seizing the chance' (a bit like ISI) or through 'development by invitation' (having the TNCs do it for you).

It is, if you like, a kind of international social mobility theory, in which the 'actors' are national economies. And crucially, as with any social mobility model, the existence of some opportunities for mobility does *not* imply that the entire system is an open one. On the contrary, in both cases, certain kinds of mobility are compatible with and even reinforce an overall *structure* which is hierarchical and unequal.

Other Marxists of course, like Warren, take an opposite view and see capitalist growth and development proceeding virtually all over the Third World. Time will tell who is right. A crucial test case will be whether the next 'rung' of Third World countries below the NICs – Malaysia or Indonesia, Peru or Colombia, say – will be able to follow the Brazils or Taiwans, and move on from low-wage textiles and assembly into diversified but increasingly balanced national economies.

So, for some on the right, the experience of the NICs simply goes to show that the market knows best. But that conveniently ignores the considerable role of the state in almost all NICs: providing grants and incentives, setting up actual enterprises, allocating credit and investment funds, controlling (or suppressing) wage negotiations, developing technology, carefully selecting foreign investment, seeking out markets – all this in addition to the usual fiscal and monetary policies.

Meanwhile, on the left, some try to salvage a modified dependency position with concepts like the *new international division of labour*. As discussed above, this implies that basically TNCs and developed countries still rule the roost; and if today some industrialization is taking place in the Third World, it's only because that suits them. The essential nature of the world system has not changed. Or has it?

The NICs, however, do seem to be doing something about it. Moreover, and crucially, on closer inspection at least part of what they are doing cannot simply be attributed to the interests of the already developed countries. On the contrary, there are often contradictions and clashes of interest. For example, South Korea's steel, construction and ship-building industries are a real threat to established producers.

Part of the response to this would be to say that this is because TNCs have no national interest. They go where the profits are, even if that means relocating part or even whole industries overseas, and hence harming their own original national economy (as has arguably been the practice of many British TNCs in recent years). However, this is not the whole picture. Third World 'actors' include not only national governments but also, increasingly, *their own TNCs* – which are a growing force on the world scene, and major investors in their own right (albeit often with support from their governments) in other countries' EPZs.

Perhaps it is helpful then to consider dependency theory as indicating not a total system and straitjacket, so much as a linked series of obstacles which are very difficult to overcome – but which nonetheless certain actors may be able to deal with. At all events, it becomes increasingly difficult to categorize Third World strategies of the 1980s into neat boxes: capitalism vs socialism, or even export-orientation vs import-substituting industrialization.

Sutcliffe Reconsiders

Bob Sutcliffe, whose 1971 study was cited earlier (p. 28), has recently reviewed the position as he sees it almost fifteen years on (in Kaplinsky, 1984). To recap, he defined an industrialized country as one where the industrial sector: (i) contributes at least 25% of GDP (gross domestic product); (ii) consists 60% or more of manufacturing; and (iii) employs more than 10% of the population. Not many new countries, he notes, have passed his threefold 'test' of industrialization since then. Uruguay, Israel, Yugoslavia and Portugal have crossed the borderline to join those that were already there (Western and Eastern Europe, North America, Japan, Australasia, Argentina, Hong Kong, Malta and Singapore). But the only wholly new arrivals are South Korea and probably Taiwan. Others, NICs and near NICs, which might pass on the first two (sectoral) criteria fail on the third, industrial *employment*.

This leads Sutcliffe to question over-optimistic views, such as Warren's, of industrialization as a *general* process in the Third World. For one thing, the North-South 'gap' in manufacturing output per head remains wide. A NIC like South Korea has certainly undergone structural change: in terms of percent of labour force in and the sectoral share of industry, it appears as industrialized as the UK. Yet its manufacturing output per head in 1978 was $621, compared with the UK's $2,667. From such data Sutcliffe concludes that real structural industrialization can take place at much lower rates of labour productivity than happened in the West.

However, secondly, some alleged structural shifts from agriculture to industry are misleading, since they may simply indicate bad *agricultural* performance. As Sutcliffe caustically notes, ' "industrialization'' here is a sign not of economic advance but of economic decline' (1984, p. 127). Thirdly, Sutcliffe detects a complicated set of trends at work which are best quoted in his own words:

> A form of industrialization has been taking place in quite a widespread manner. But in many countries it is composed of different elements which are not homogeneous and do not unambiguously represent economic modernisation . . . What seems to be happening is that modern industry is growing at high and rising productivity levels and at the same time small-scale, more primitive industry survives at low, possibly declining productivity levels, but provides a meagre living for a growing share of the people. What may be occurring therefore is a process of internal polarisation, one which is more complex and extreme . . . and one which is very different from what took place in the successful indus-trializations of the past. (1984, pp. 128–129)

More broadly and reflectively, Sutcliffe also considers something to which we should now turn our attention: namely, the costs of industrialization.

The Costs of Industrialization

As Barrington Moore (1966) has gloomily noted, there is no evidence that the majority of people anywhere have ever actively wanted an industrial society, and plenty that they have not. Whatever its long-run material and other benefits, industrialization *at the time* is a costly process: economically, politically and culturally.

As an *economic* process, first of all, industrialization by definition involves shifting the balance from consumption to investment, often at a high rate and for a long period. It is, literally, a case of jam today versus jam tomorrow; and, if the latter is chosen, people must tighten their belts as they invest in the future. This iron necessity applies equally to capitalist and socialist regimes. Doubtless as a result, indus-trialization so far has everywhere been associated with *political* authoritarianism. We should think of it, not so much as an abstract social *process*, but a definite *project*: as something which some people do at the expense of others.

The choices and conflicts which arise here can be viewed in two linked ways. In part, they are *generational*: one generation (or part of it) foregoes consumption (i.e. gives up goodies), in order that the investment thus created may enable their children (or grandchildren) to consume more and better than they ever could have, without that sacrifice. But industrialization is also very much a *class* question. By definition, in societies which are initially agrarian it is peasants who get squeezed, sometimes mercilessly: by enclosures in England, by collectivization and requisitions in the USSR. As these examples may suggest, who does the squeezing can vary. Moore's account, as we saw, found several possible combinations and alliances of rising bourgeoisie, modernizing sections of old rural oligarchies, and so on. As for the link between generation and class, this consists in *social mobility*. Not least among the tragic ironies of Soviet industrialization in the 1930s was that the 'workers' on whose behalf the 'peasants' were smashed were in most cases the sons and daughters, brothers and sisters of those same peasants.

Industrialization also has its *cultural* costs. Old ways are shattered, or eroded. Small-scale activities become uneconomic and disappear. A brash new smoky squalid urban industrial society thrusts its way onto centre stage, while the old rural world is pushed to the margins. The impersonal replaces the personal, community is superseded by organization. There are echoes here of the famous themes of Nisbet's *The Sociological Tradition* (1967), which identified precisely these such unprecedented changes as provoking the reflections out of which sociology itself was born.

There is of course another side to all this. Modernization theorists, and not only they, would retort that whatever the rigours of the 'steep ascent' the eventual plateau of industrial society is well worth it. At least since 1945, Western societies have enjoyed a combination of economic well-being, political democracy, and cultural breadth which is historically quite without precedent. None of this would have been possible without industrialization. Sacrifice there certainly was, but it wasn't in vain. And the rest of the world both can have and is entitled to share the same benefits.

Still, as we have seen this process is far from being problem-free. Perhaps it is not too utopian to suppose that by now, after some 200 years of global industrialization, we could learn some lessons and apply them to the process in the future. It is already clear that there is no single royal road to industrialization. Different countries vary widely in their size, climate, and resource endowments, as well as their history, social structure and type of political regime. The balance of market and planning may vary considerably; althouth any industrialization process nowadays (whatever the monetarists say) is likely to involve a good deal of state intervention.

Nor is it always necessary – or even possible, in some countries – any more to 'sacrifice' agriculture to industry. A steelworks in every country may not be a feasible goal. Some smaller agrarian countries might do better to concentrate on feeding themselves and developing agro-industries. In technology, too, there are choices. Thanks to the work of E. F. Schumacher (1974), it is increasingly recognized that 'small is beautiful'. Or can be, since it would be wrong to generalize. But relatively small-scale production and organization may be appropriate in specific cases. In particular, Third World countries where labour is abundant may well at first choose relatively labour-intensive, 'older' or intermediate technology, rather than the very latest expensive machinery which creates hardly any jobs.

Finally, we should note the paradox of being a 'late developer'. On the one hand, the firstcomers have so carved up the world and ensconced themselves within it that it sometimes seems as if newcomers can hardly get a look in. On the other hand, just as technologically nobody has to re-invent the wheel, socially too it should be possible (at least in principle) for today's would-be developers to take a long, hard look at the harsher sides of earlier industrialization experiences: to learn something from their mistakes, and to make choices at once more purposive and less brutal.

But is it Possible? – The Ecological Dimension

With this stark question, Goldthorpe (1984) opens his own chapter on a set of considerations which can scarcely be ignored (though they all too often have been) in any discussion of industrialization. Irrespective of dependency arguments about socio-political blockages to industrialization, and criticisms of the human costs of the process, are there *ecological* constraints which in any case rule out any prospect of a world-wide industrial society?

Some have certainly argued so, in no uncertain terms. Thus the Ehrlichs state baldly that 'our environment cannot stand "world industrialization" '. And they do not hesitate to grasp the nettle: 'Most of these countries [LDCs] will never, under any conceivable circumstances, be "developed" in the sense in which the United States is today. They could quite accurately be called the "never-to-be-developed" countries' (quoted in Goldthorpe, 1984, p. 106). On the other hand, no less robust opinions can be found which dismiss such views, and stress the possibilities for global abundance. Although there is no space for a detailed rehearsal of all the arguments here, we shall follow Goldthorpe in breaking the issue down into four distinct areas: pollution, food, non-renewable resources, and energy.

That *pollution* is frequently a local problem is undeniable, especially in the early stages of any country's industrialization where there are often all too few controls on such 'externalities' as the dumping of wastes. For it to be a *global* problem involves further claims; e.g. that vast increases in energy consumption would alter the heat balance and the climate, or that cumulative discharge of wastes may irreversibly affect ecological cycles. There is no clear evidence yet, thankfully, for such global changes. Local problems, however, are unfortunately only too familiar, and require constant vigilance on the part of governments and pressure groups to prevent a given industry's 'external' costs being dumped on outsiders and future generations. Alas, in this business of 'fouling one's own nest' it is not infrequently governments themselves who are among the worst offenders.

Food is not strictly a matter of industrialization, but there are at least two important links. First, an increasingly industrialized globe needs to be fed. In the past there has been much alarm about this, as expressed in books with titles like *Famine 1975!* The fact this date has after all come and gone suggests, as Goldthorpe puts it, that the Malthusian spectre has receded. As discussed elsewhere in this book, the Green Revolution (whatever its economic and social implications) has *technically* solved the *global* food problem. Shortages that remain, however appalling (e.g. the 1984/5 famine in Ethiopia), are largely localized to one continent, Africa. Or is this too complacent? For the second issue here concern the *nature* of this agricultural success, itself highly 'industrialized' and based on resource-expensive fertilizers, which some critics maintain is exhausting the soil.

This leads into the question of non-renewable *resources*. (Even *renewable* resources, it should be noted, can be at risk: forests are being torn down as far apart as Indonesia and the Brazilian Amazon, and it is reckoned that each *minute* some 14 hectares of tropical rainforest are being lost to the world (Redclift, 1984, p. 26)). Mineral endowments, in contrast to agricultural, are literally finite. The issue is therefore threefold. First, at the moment new resources are still being discovered, but this process will obviously reach its limit eventually. Secondly, even used mineral resources are not lost. As Goldthorpe has said, all the iron that there ever was in the earth is still there; in other words, the process of recycling 'scrap' is likely to become relatively more economical. Thirdly, in this as in other aspects it is obviously prudent to seek where possible to develop new technologies, which minimize dependence on non-renewable resources.

Much the same applies to *energy*. In the most notorious case, oil, reaction to the OPEC price increases since 1973 has already led to many industrial processes becoming somewhat less oil-dependent. Other fossil fuels remain much more abundant: thus only 1–2% of available coal has yet been extracted. Nuclear energy is as yet expensive, and carries political and social risks. But the future for the Third World may well lie in developing wind, tidal and solar power, which are inexhaustible as long as the sun continues to be – although effective technologies for harnessing these scarcely exist as yet.

This brief review of ecological factors affecting industrialization should encourage neither alarmism nor complacency. Ecological issues were neglected for a long time, but the very publicity and awareness they now raise gives some hope of solutions being found.

Finally, in a sociological text it would be wrong not to make a brief comment on ecology as *social* theory. Ecological debates on both sides have been bedevilled by heavy doses of ideology. The fact that some of us in the West are feeling a certain disenchantment and boredom with our industrial civilization, from which we have gained so much, is hardly a good reason to deny its benefits to a Third World which has yet to experience this and may badly want to. Those in the West who want to go 'back to nature' are liable to forget, not only that this 'Nature' is not so much a reality as a cultural concept like any other, but also that many in the Third World would like nothing more than to get *away* from nature – or at least from being at its mercy in terms of food, shelter, and life-chances generally.

Conversely, ecological optimists often seem guilty of an arrogant complacency, as well as projecting from past 'success' to assume that nothing can ever run out or go radically wrong. Like everything else, these ecological issues turn out to be empirical questions, with no uniform or fixed answers. It is something that has to be watched.

Chapter Four
Urbanization

Definitions

Probably we all think we know what a town is, even more so a city. Nevertheless, as Hardiman and Midgley (1982) observe, there are a lot of problems of definition and comparison in this field. There is no single agreed usage for such terms as 'town', 'city', 'metropolis', etc. let alone for more theory-laden words like 'urbanism' and 'urbanization'. Four particular problems may be mentioned.

In the first place, different countries may use different and arbitrary measures of what's urban and what isn't, thus making cross-national comparisons of urbanization very hazardous. Secondly, even where a minimum figure is agreed for a settlement to count as urban, it is often too low, as the average size of *all* settlements continues to increase. Once, a population of 2000 might have served to distinguish an urban place. Today, it is more likely to mean a biggish village – yet this figure is still sometimes used as a threshold of urbanism. Thirdly, for obvious reasons, definitions of cities tend to be related to administrative boundaries. Yet this too can be sociologically misleading. With continued growth, cities tend to overspill their boundaries. Should we regard the eastern seaboards of the USA and Japan as a series of cities, or as each a gigantic sprawling megalopolis? Finally, whatever threshold you use there will be bumps and lumps in the figures, as rising populations continually entail the redefinition overnight of a 'village' of 19,999 into a town of 20,001.

Kingsley Davis (cited in Hardiman and Midgley, 1982, p. 126ff) has done more than most to try to bring statistical and conceptual order to this chaos. His suggested threshold definitions of 20,000 for an 'urban place' and 100,000 for a city are now widely used, e.g. by UN agencies.

Davis defines 'urbanization' as a growth in the proportion of the country's population living in cities. Thus cities can grow in size without urbanization occurring if the rural population increases at an even greater rate. This is an important point. In Europe urbanization developed rapidly due to massive rural-urban migration. In the Third World urbanization is much slower because rural populations continue to rise rapidly despite migration to the cities.

Urbanization Historically

There have been cities for at least 5000 years, in both what are now the developed and underdeveloped worlds. Some were very large. According to Goldthorpe (1984), Rome at the height of its power around 150 AD had about a million inhabitants, and presided over an empire some 10% of whose 100 million population were urbanized. Yet, by the 9th century, Rome itself had shrunk to a mere 20,000, and would not reach a million again until this century. This shows one difference between the pre-industrial and the modern city. The former quite often fluctuated in size, due to war or natural disaster. In the latter, by contrast, with rare exceptions (and apart from the process of suburbanization in the First World, itself arguably a form of further urbanization rather than a counter-trend) the movement is strictly one way: in and up, often at rapid rates.

Historically, like today, the biggest cities of all have often been in the Third World. China in the thirteenth century had several urban centres each with over a million inhabitants. Nonetheless, such pre-industrial cities typically still contained only a small percentage of their countries' total population. And, almost by definition, their function in the societies tended to be as commerical, administrative or military centres rather than any 'industrial' role.

England, the first industrial nation, was also the first to urbanize. An urban majority was reached as early as 1851, and fifty years later the UK was still the world's only predominantly urbanized society. The British figure peaked at over 80% in 1951, but according to Goldthorpe has fallen slightly since because of the rise of commuting. Hardiman and Midgley (1982) by contrast, quote a still higher figure of 91% urbanized for the UK in 1980: a discrepancy doubtless due to differences of definition as outlined in the previous section.

Facts and Figures

Urbanization as a global process is a product of the twentieth century, and indeed largely of the latter half of that century. As recently as 1960, only 20% of a world population of 3 billion lived in cities. Even this, however, reflected a massive increase (both absolutely, and in percentage terms) during the epoch of the Industrial Revolution. In 1800, only 1.7% of the world's 900 million people lived in cities; so a century and a half later, while the total population had increased three-fold, city-dwellers were almost *forty* times more numerous (up from 15 to 590 million approximately). Such is urbanization, in Davis' sense.

And urban growth continues apace. By 1980, 41% of the world's population was urban, meaning some 1,560 million people. During the 1970s, too, the numerical balance shifted to the Third World: so the 'typical' urbanite in our world lives not in the West but in the South. These processes will continue, such that a majority of *all* the world's people will be urban by the year 2000. Overall, between 1900 and 1975, while world population rose two and a half times (1,600 to 4,000 million), urban numbers multiplied no less than tenfold (150 to 1,500 million).

Distribution by continent remains uneven, however. As of 1980, both Asia and Africa had urban populations still under 30%. The African figure was slightly ahead of Asia's, and it is indeed in Africa that the world's fastest urban growth is currently taking place. However, because it starts from the lowest base-lines, this does not yet show up very much in overall size or percentages. Within Asia, there is much variation. Urbanization is highest in West and East Asia (the latter of course including two city-states, Hong Kong and Singapore), and lowest in South Asia. Latin America, by contrast was already 50% urbanized by 1960. The 1980 figure approaches 65%, and the projection for 2000 is 75% – virtually on a par with that in the North.

This higher Latin American urbanization reflects the cumulative effect of a high rate of natural increase within cities plus a good deal of continuing rural-urban migration. And it is worth mentioning that this continent contains the monster of them all: Mexico City, already esti-mated to have some 16 million people, and scheduled to rise by the end of the century to a staggering 25 million – i.e. more than most entire countries!

Third World Urbanization

As always, however, facts do not speak for themselves. It is time to begin to try to link all these figures to major analytical debates. And here, as ever, one of the main bones of contention between modern-ization and dependency approaches concerns 'recapitulation'. Is the Third World's urbanization following the pattern of the West's, such that we may accurately speak of a single global process? There are a number of complex issues and factors here, and they are admirably summarized by Hardiman and Midgley (1982, p. 132ff). We might say that the South's urbanization, paradoxically, is both more and less than – but, in either case, significantly divergent from -- the North's. On the one hand, the pace of urban growth in the Third World today is historically unprecedented, with rates of growth typically twice as fast as they were in late 19th century Europe. On the other hand, this rapid urban *growth* goes along with relatively *low* rates of urbanization (remember Davis' definition). The clue is that, because Third World *rural* populations are also increasing rapidly, the overall proportion of the population living in cities increases slowly compared to 19th century Europe.

Putting it another way, much (probably most) Third World urban growth is due more to natural increase than to migration. Davis notes that today's cities in LDCs have high fertility and low mortality, whereas in 19th century Europe both were high (hence rates of natural increase, as distinct from immigration, were relatively lower – at least at first). Muddying the waters, Todaro points out an 'interference' factor: high urban natural increase may itself be attributable to the age-structure of migrant populations, many of whom are young adults at the peak of their fertility. Besides, as mentioned above, some Third World urban 'growth' is simply statistical reclassification. The pitfalls are many.

Two major differences remain to be mentioned: one quantitative, the other qualitative. Third World cities tend to be fewer and bigger rather than many and smaller. A rather common extreme, arguably specific to the ex-colonial Third World, is what Linsky called the 'primate city': a single city (normally the capital), many times larger than the next biggest, and not infrequently containing a substantial percentage of an overall national population which may not itself be all that large.

Finally, and most notoriously, what makes Third World urban-ization different is that (unlike in the West) it has often *not* been accompanied by industrialization. Rather than an expansion of classic industrial factory work, the cities of the South have instead come to feature massively swollen 'tertiary' or 'service' sectors, in which millions of people earn a precarious living in an astonishing variety of ways – relatively few of which, however, involve production, at least in any large scale context.

As we have seen there are contentious general issues here. Not a single Third World country is totally devoid of factories, and some have substantial urban industrial sectors. But in many countries this 'formal sector' seems relatively small by comparison: whether looking back to how it happened in Europe, or looking sideways to the much larger 'informal sector' which seems so distinctively to characterize the contemporary urban explosion in the Third World. Let us now examine this more closely.

The Informal Sector: What's in a Name?

The terms use to refer to some Third World urban dwellers have changed significantly. Two decades ago, when the sociological distinctiveness of these new Third World urbanites was first becoming clear, some referred to them as a 'lumpen-proletariat'. This Marxist term implies socially and politically unstable sections – beggars, hustlers, prostitutes, and so forth – marginal to mainstream economic life and without revolutionary potential. Others, like Fanon, reversed the politics of this view. It was the very marginality and indeed poverty of these, the 'wretched of the earth', which made them a 'revolutionary force', along with peasants, but *unlike* (contradicting Marx) the tiny proletariat proper, so small and privileged in the Third World as to constitute a 'labour aristocracy'.

Such sweeping visions tended to precede rather than follow empirical investigation. Admittedly, it was (and perhaps still is) understandable if observers have nightmares about just how Third World cities are going to cope with so many people, in the absence of widespread industrialization. But the evidence suggests both more stable social structures, a wider range of economic activities, and less radical politics than in the Fanonist vision. As a result, from the early 1970s a rather different and at first sight more neutral term, the 'informal sector', became prevalent – although this too has had its critics.

Bromley (1978) provides a useful ideal-type of this model of the urban economy, in terms of seven criteria. The *informal sector* is characterized by: ease of entry, indigenous resources, family ownership, small scale, labour-intensive or adapted technology, skills acquired outside the formal school system, and unregulated and often highly competitive markets. The *formal sector*, by contrast, is in each respect the opposite: difficult to get into, often using overseas resources, corporately owned, large scale, with capital-intensive and often imported technology, formally obtained (often expatriate) skills, and operating in highly protected quasi-monopolistic markets.

Such an approach has had the merit of encouraging both more research on the informal sector by academics, and a less negative attitude towards it by governments. For obvious reasons the informal

sector tends not to show up in official statistics, and sometimes operates
at or beyond the margins of legality. Hence the official mind tends to
classify it as a problem, and sometimes to act accordingly – in rounding
up or harassing street-vendors, in demolishing squatter settlements,
expelling 'vagrants' back to the countryside, and so on. Against this,
the International Labour Office in particular in a series of reports
during the 1970s urged the merits of the informal sector, seeing it as
more of a solution than a problem, providing goods and services to fill
the gaps in the less flexible formal sector, and generally keeping people
out of mischief.

Nevertheless, the term 'informal sector' itself has attracted
increasing criticism. Once again Bromley (1978) provides a convenient
summary. The model is too dualistic: we need more than just the two
categories 'formal' and 'informal', probably a continuum. It also
falsely implies separateness of the two sectors: it downplays their interaction, and indeed the possible domination of one sector by another.
This is important, because much field research suggests that in various
ways the informal sector (directly or indirectly, and consciously or
otherwise) is bound in with and serves the formal sector. For example,
research carried out on a rubbish dump (literally!) in the Colombian
city of Cali showed how waste paper collected by scavengers eventually
found its way, through a series of middlemen, to one of the biggest
paper mills in the country for recycling (Birkbeck in Bromley and
Gerry, 1979).

Bromley is also worried about what the term 'informal sector' lumps
together, and equally what it splits up or leaves out. In policy terms, the
use of a single term might imply that a single government approach will
do for diverse areas of the informal sector such as furniture, fireworks,
foodstuffs, and prostitutes – which is unlikely. Related to this is a
simplistic assumption that, if only policy makers will take heed, the
informal sector will thrive and hence disappear as such (by becoming
formal!). Analytically, meanwhile, the phrase confuses different sorts
of units: neighbourhoods, households, individuals, activities, and
enterprises. Only the last, says Bromley, are at all likely to be
'either/or' (formal or informal). All the rest are liable to be
'both . . . and', with much overlapping. And this goes along with the
false equation of the informal sector as identical to the urban poor. In
reality, not all the poor are in the informal sector, and by no means is
everybody in the informal sector necessarily poor.

Finally, in this critique, there is what the term 'informal sector'
leaves out. Two important things, according to Bromley. One is the
countryside; where there are similar and indeed often linked activities

(artisans, petty traders, etc.) – yet who in the rural context are often perversely regarded as 'traditional'. The other is the State: here, as so often in development studies, an implicit but unstated subject and key actor, which really ought to be painted in to complete the picture – even if it is also the painter.

If not 'informal sector', what else should we call it? Those concerned to apply Marxist economic categories (often going beyond, or even against, dependency theory in order to work out the empirical micro-implications) have lately used terms such as *petty commodity producer* in both urban and rural contexts – in the latter case preferring this term to the analytically vague word 'peasants'. A broader-based term is offered by Bromley and Gerry, namely *'casual work'*. They define this as 'any way of making a living which lacks a moderate degree of security of income and employment', whether productive or not, working for oneself or others, legally or otherwise.

One advantage of this term is that it can cope with the range of *forms* of employment found in Third World cities, to which the contrast of wage labour 'versus' self-employment does scant justice. Such inter-mediate forms include: short-term or 'casual' waged work (by the day, week, month, or season); 'disguised' wage-work (e.g. out-work, or commission sellers); and 'dependent' work (dependent, that is, on larger, 'formal' enterprises for anything from credit and materials to premises and sales outlets).

Even so, I dare say that despite its theoretical shortcomings the term 'informal sector' (rather like the equally criticized term 'underdevelopment' itself) will survive. The real point, as always, is to be aware of the different analytical issues that arise from this empirically and concep-tually complex yet fascinating area.

Housing and Settlements: Slums of Hope?

The previous section focussed on aspects of *work*; and we noted that it was wrong to equate this sector with others, such as housing, in the rather blurry way that a term like 'informal sector' might imply. So having looked at work in its own right, we must now do the same for housing and settlement.

Everyone has seen pictures of shanty-towns: barrios, favelas, bidon-villes, bustees – the names are as numerous as the countries where they exist, which in effect means virtually the entire Third World. And there is, of course, substantial overlap with the informal sector. Many millions who have no regular job, equally have no 'regular' housing; for both work and shelter they fend for themselves. Yet in both spheres of life, the result is social structures both more organized and systematic than the chaotic randomness which may be the observer's first impression.

One problem, however, is that in few areas of the sociology of development are approaches quite so coloured by the observer's biasses. As Hardiman and Midgley (1982) note, sociology as a dis-cipline tends to have anti-urban prejudices in any case, at least in its implicit nostalgia for alleged lost 'community'. So it was predictable that many, whether from a modernization or dependency perspective, should hasten to categorize Third World slums under the heading of social pathology. Phrases like Oscar Lewis' famous 'culture of poverty' may have different explanatory force from the preferred dependency term 'marginality', in that (to oversimplify) the former blames the victim while the latter blames the system. Yet both share an implicitly negative attitude: this is a social problem.

Against this view, John Turner maintains that 'the slum is not a problem . . . but a viable solution to the problems of rapid urbaniz-ation' (Hardiman and Midgley, 1982, p. 143). Philosophically Turner is an anarchist, which at least lets in a bit of ideological fresh air. 'Spontaneous settlements' – a more neutral term than 'slums' – do a job: they offer cheap accommodation, provide access to employment, and generally give the new migrant a foothold in the city. What's more, by definition these are settlements in which people do their own thing rather than have things done to them (whether for or against them). Turner is all for self-help, both as individual and collective action. Thus, to take an actual example from Ecuador, squatters might set up house right on a city garbage dump where they work, and then petition the municipal authorities to provide such services as standpipes and electricity.

Turner's views are controversial, and all the issues are complex. It's hard not to sympathize with Lloyd's (1979) view that the notion of 'marginality' is vague to the point of uselessness, if (say) up to 75% of the urban population are to be classed as 'marginal'! As for the 'culture of poverty', one can make two points. Empirical variation is likely: some slums may be as Oscar Lewis described in Puerto Rico, while others seem preoccupied with self-improvement. Besides, it isn't a point of culture 'versus' structure: they may well be interdependent.

There is also empirical evidence that many slum dwellers are neither disorganized, apathetic, or even especially radical. Voluntary associ-ations (often ethnic-based) to help new migrants on arrival in the city have a long history all over the Third World. And the desire to 'get on', even in appalling material circumstances, seems often as powerful as that for radical change. But generalizations are hazardous. In a sense the Third World slum, like the informal sector, is *both* a problem *and* a solution. Stressing the often amazing resourcefulness of the people and communities involved is helpful, insofar as it checks governments from having a jaundiced and hostile attitude – especially if, as so often, the State has nothing positive to offer once it has bulldozed the shanties or driven the hawkers off the streets (probably they'll both be back in the morning). And yet to praise people's resourcefulness must not entail complacency about their adversity, such that the government feels let off the hook. Ultimately, and despite the formidable difficulties, the resources and planning necessary to provide even a halfway decent urban environment – be it for housing, work, travel, or whatever – can only come from the state.

Internal Migration and Social Classes

Movement by individuals or households between countries – *international* migration – is a major factor of modern society, as the ethnic profile of the postwar UK illustrates. Still more widespread, and arguably more fundamental, is *internal* migration: movement within national boundaries, almost always meaning from country to town. Although in industrialized countries this has virtually ceased as a systematic social process, it was of great historical importance in its time. In the Third World today, notwithstanding that much urban growth arises from natural increase rather than migration, the latter is a major social movement – literally! – and has been extensively studied. We want to know who migrates, how, and why, and with what consequences (for themselves, and for society as a whole).

Inevitably over-generalizing; migrants tend to be young unmarried adults. Mostly, they are male; and even if they are not (as in Latin America), men tend to migrate before women. Some studies have found that migrants have above-average education levels, or that they come from middle-income groups, rather than the very poorest or richest. Reasons for migration can involve all sorts of combinations of 'push' and 'pull'. We in the West tend to romanticize the countryside, but many in the Third World have good reason to try to get away from land scarcity, poverty, underemployment, a general lack of opportunities, or in extreme cases famine or violence. On the other side of the coin, despite the risks of urban life, people are lured by the possibilities which it offers, at least in principle and for some: better education, health, social services, living standards; perhaps a job, at all events some way of making ends meet. And, vaguer but just as real: the lure of the bright lights, the excitement (however enervating) of modernity, its open-endedness compared with what Marx witheringly called 'the idiocy of rural life'.

So they come. *How* they come is interesting, and seems to indicate differences from as well as similarities to the 'same' processes in the West. The main difference can best be summarized in Marxist terms. Unlike in the West, proletarianization in the Third World is far from complete, and shows every sign of remaining that way. People do not lose their links with the land entirely, or only very slowly. Individuals and especially households pursue complex strategies and create intricate patterns, to the despair of those who would like to find classes in neat clear-cut boxes. Sometimes there is *step* migration: first to a local small town, then on to a larger city. Sometimes there is *seasonal* migration, by the year or shorter and longer periods. Importantly, not all migration is rural-urban (or the return flows). Intra-rural migration is becoming more common. People have long gone to work for plantations; now they go to work for agri-businesses, and a country like Mexico has been described as having vast seasonal armies of millions of migrant labourers, roaming the countryside in search of employment.

The links to theory are interesting here, and may be worth spelling out. To describe what is going on at a macro-level, the appropriate broad categories seem to me to be Marxist ones like proletarianization (or lack of it) and accumulation. Nevertheless, the sheer complexity (empirical and analytical) of the *actual* social relations involved poses great challenges for a Marxist approach. To find definite classes, or even classes definitely in formation, let alone to impute particular forms of political consciousness and predict particular kinds of political action – all this is hazardous, and certainly can't be done from first principles. Rather, one must first go out and look.

Chapter Five

Rural Development

Facts and Figures

Despite growing urbanization, the great majority of the Third World's population – over 2 billion people – still lives in the countryside. Moreover, despite rural-urban migration, this figure is increasing in *absolute* terms by an average of some 2% p.a., even while the relative proportion of rural inhabitants in total population declines. By continent, only in Latin America are rural dwellers a minority, outnumbered in 1985 by an estimated 2:1. Yet even here their *numbers* are increasing in almost all countries. In Africa and Asia, by contrast, the proportions are more or less reversed, with some 70% of the population still rural. (Needless to say, these are averages; figures for individual countries may differ widely.)

While we in the West tend to sentimentalize the countryside, in the Third World rural life often means poverty. Almost three quarters of the global poor (550 mn out of 750 mn) live in rural areas (Hardiman and Midgley, 1982). Another striking statistic of global difference concerns *agricultural productivity*, especially in relation to food. A single farmer in the USA feeds, on average, 65 people. In some parts of the Third World (especially Africa) by contrast, even countries which are overwhelmingly agrarian (i.e. agriculture is almost all there is, or all that anybody does) cannot feed themselves. In fact, according to Adamson (1984) the nature of the global food problem is often misunderstood. For one thing, there isn't a *global* food problem. World grain production reached record levels in 1984; it grew by 7% as against 1983, while population grew 2%. Each of us needs the equivalent of some 250 kg of grain per year; the 1984 harvest yielded 50% *more* than this, for every person in the world.

The catch, of course, lies in the *distribution* and *use* of the grains grown. Europe and North America between them produced enough to feed the entire world. Asia and Latin America produced enough to feed themselves; Africa, however, only produced 50% of its grain needs. And where did the North's surplus in fact go? A breakdown of the US figure reveals that 13% was eaten directly, 27% was sold commercially overseas, while 20% went to replanting and storing (the latter contributing to pile yet higher the infamous 'mountains' of food surplus possessed by both the USA and the EEC). I have left till last the largest and smallest figures. 40% of US grain went for cattle feed. And just 0.5% went as aid to the hungry.

Even so, Adamson argues against the popular myth that half the world's population is starving. On the contrary, the proportion of those who are *overfed* (2%) is greater than those visibly under-nourished (less than 1% – although this still represents tens of millions of hungry human beings). Some 90% of the world's population are at least tolerably well fed. But that still leaves 10%, or over 450 million, who are not.

Variations by Region

As Hardiman and Midgley note (1982, p.102 ff), patterns of access to and control over land vary widely from place to place. *Latin America* exhibits an extraordinary range of scales and types of land ownership and tenure. Very large and often inefficient *latifundia*, large estates where social relations may be seemingly feudal (although the aptness of this term is hotly controversial), exist alongside and dominate tiny *minifundia* (very small family farms). Land and labour productivity is low, technology is poor, and large numbers of small producers are in practice dependent on their landlord – whether providing unpaid labour, or as sharecroppers (handing over a portion of the crop), but in either case lacking basic security of tenure. Alongside this there also exist more modern and better capitalized farms, both family-sized and larger.

The *Asian* picture is significantly different. Although land concentration is high (i.e. smallholdings being grouped together in larger units), what counts as a 'large' unit is much smaller than in Latin America. Population density is much greater, making land scarcity the critical problem (unlike in Latin America or Africa, where 'colonization' in the geographers' sense – i.e. bringing new land under cultivation – is still a widely available option). Absentee landlords are numerous, and resulting tenancy and sharecropping arrangements are at once onerous but also more 'decentralized' than in Latin America. Technology and hence land and labour productivity is poor, while production is labour-intensive and more for subsistence than export. Rural poverty is a major problem, especially in South Asia, as illustrated in the rise of moneylenders and the often permanent indebtedness of very many people.

One reason for the severity of Asia's problems is the breakdown of traditional agrarian relations under the impact of the colonial introduction of private property in land. In *Africa*, by contrast, precapitalist forms of customary tenure are still found to some extent. This (plus low population density) has helped prevent land concentration and inequality on the scale experienced elsewhere in the Third World. On the other hand, productivity and technology alike are very low. Much, probably most African agriculture still revolves around humans wielding hoes, rather than oxen drawing ploughs – let alone tractors. There is still much shifting cultivation (so-called 'slash and burn'). And ironically, although subsistence agriculture still predominates, it is Africa alone of the Third World's continents which for the most part is chronically (and increasingly) unable to feed itself; as witness the famines of the Sahel and, more recently, Ethiopia.

Rural Communities: an Ideal-type?

Modernization and dependency theorists are apt to disagree dramatically about how we should conceptualize rural communities in the Third World today. For the former, tradition still largely holds sway, obstacles to progress are internal, and cultural characteristics are particularly problematical. For the latter, by contrast, the main problem is the 'modern' (but non-beneficial) externally imposed economic constraints of capitalism.

Hardiman and Midgley (1982) to some extent try to have it both ways. They begin by constructing a sort of Weberian 'ideal-type'. Rural communities are *small-scale* societies, often not very densely populated, in which face-to-face interaction looms large, yet the scope of individuality is limited. Family and *kinship* are omnipresent and multifunctional: rather than being just one sphere of life among others (and a declining one at that), kinship permeates and links all aspects of society – economic, political, juridical, religious, and social welfare. *Territory* is important both instrumentally and symbolically. *Means of production* are technically simple; and the *division of labour* is based principally on age and sex. Methods of cultivation are traditional, hence *labour-intensive*, depending mainly on inputs of human energy.

The primary goal of production is *subsistence*; any cash crops are secondary, and self-sufficiency is the goal. Culturally, *ritual* is important: a harsh environment breeds a sense of being at the mercy of nature, fatalism, superstition, and supernaturalism – albeit not necessarily excluding scientific beliefs and practices. Finally, economic self-sufficiency has its political and 'jural' counterparts, inasmuch as traditional communities have little *separation of spheres* between (e.g.) executive, legislative and judicial realms.

Hardiman and Midgley go on to add qualifications to this picture. They stress that such 'communities' were not and are not homogeneous, consensual and static, but rather experience differentiation and conflicts – even before the impact of 'social change'. Nonetheless, I think there are real pitfalls in setting up the problem in this way. The most obvious risk is *over-generalization*. Some of these characteristics, especially the first and last, might fit pre-colonial Africa – but would scarcely do for the civilizations of East and South Asia, densely populated and long since linked to a wider state. Secondly, the content of this ideal-type is heavily *Durkheimian*: tradition is implicitly equated with simplicity, diffuseness, and lack of differentiation. Yet much anthropological evidence has brought out the intricacy and complexity of social relations, even in small-scale societies with low levels of technology.

Above all, as with any attempts to construct the 'traditional', what is in question is its precise resemblance to the Third World *today*. Rather like those anthropologists who began with the notion of 'tribe', and then found that with urban migration they had a self-inflicted conceptual problem of 'detribalization', it is perhaps an unwise procedure to begin with a supposed pre-existent reality and only later introduce 'change' from the outside. Granted, that may be the way it actually happened. But surely what we need to do today is to analyse the actual complex and mixed social forms we find in the rural Third World, in terms of their own dynamics and reproduction. True, Hardiman and Midgley go on to look at how this earlier ideal-type is eroded by such trends as the effects of labour migration, the penetration of a cash economy, the spread of urban values, and a general increase in the number, intensity and variety of the links which tie the small community to wider national and indeed international contexts. But the very determining power of those ties inspires the methodological thought that perhaps then this would have been the place to start an analysis of present-day rural realities, rather than bring it in later.

Rural Change, Colonial and Since

By way of contrast, Johnson (1983) adopts an approach which emphasises the drastic degrees of transformation which Third World rural social structures have long since undergone, both under the impact of colonialism and subsequently. In general, colonialism profoundly affected what was grown, who was to grow it, and how. The introduction of the Western concept of *private property* in land often had a revolutionary effect (as Marx noted for India), transforming old social relations and creating new ones. Money *taxation* (by head or hut) had scarcely less drastic effects; including *labour migration* to various sources of employment (rural plantations, mines, or towns). Alternatively, the spread of commercialized *markets* sometimes presented itself to more fortunate peasants as opportunity rather than compulsion, such that they began producing *food* for these other sectors (plantations, mines, towns). More than this, some peasants began growing *cash crops*; which often brought them into competition with the large-scale *plantations* created for this purpose by colonialism.

Most of these trends continue today. The commercialization of small-scale agriculture, in particular, has a number of effects. Staple foods are increasingly being displaced by *commercial crops*; including 'luxury' grains, like wheat and (in some cases) rice, which may not meet the foods needs of those who grow them. *Land concentration* in fewer holdings means that large numbers are being *displaced* from the land, hence peasant producers are becoming more differentiated, i.e. some are becoming wealthy farmers, others poor farm labourers. The effects on *labour* are contradictory: an increasingly large agricultural *proletariat* may be simultaneously being augmented by peasants made landless and displaced by mechanization.

Johnson notes elements of persistence as well as the changes mentioned above. Many peasants still use very basic technologies and stick to well-tried practices. (So-called peasant 'conservatism' reflects the fact that, for poor small-scale producers, any innovation carries enormous risks.) Much agricultural production is still carried on by households using family labour. Most of them still produce their own food, over and above any cash crops. And there still survive, often on a large scale, such seemingly 'pre-capitalist' forms of land ownership and labour use as share-cropping and debt bondage.

This account by Johnson could be criticized as overly *economistic* (although, to be fair, her brief was to write a text unit on production). Nonetheless, I think this approach has two sociological merits. First, the sorts of things she focusses on, whether or not they 'determine' other aspects of existence, certainly form the essential framework or context within which rural Third World people must live – and over much of which they have little control. As such, this seems a sensible place to start from. Secondly, you may have noticed that almost all the factors Johnson mentions are *processes*, rather than *states*. Instead of the unavoidably static construction of ideal-types, which then (so to speak) have to be jump-started into life from some outside force, this places movement and change at the centre of the analysis – which is as it should be.

Peasants

There is no general agreement about what constitutes a peasant. It has been said that 'peasants are the majority of mankind' (Shanin, 1971, p. 238). This implies that over vast reaches of place and time, through an immense variety of cultures and social structures, hundreds of millions of people have enough in common to justify the use of a singular term to describe them. For one thing, as the root of the word implies, peasants live in the countryside. Yet it is not as simple as that, in several ways. Not all peasants live in the countryside; Bryan Roberts (1978) entitled his book on Third World urbanization: *Cities of Peasants*. (The *migration* which this refers to is discussed in a separate section.) And not all rural dwellers are peasants. Some may be agricultural labourers. Some may be 'communal cultivators', and not yet peasants (we shall return to this below). And yet others, importantly, may be landlords.

So peasants don't usually (perhaps ever) occupy the countryside alone. In fact we might say that peasants are rural dwellers with two crucial linked qualifications: (1) they are in some form of subordinate class/status relation to others; (2) they form part of some wider social/political/economic structure. We could call these *vertical* and *horizontal* linkages, respectively.

In terms of the vertical linkage, we might treat the landlord-peasant relationship as an earlier rural version of bourgeoisie and proletariat, rather as we saw Barrington Moore (1966) did. Like bourgeoisie/proletariat, landlord/peasant is of course an oversimplification of real situations which are both more complex and in motion. Complexity consists in (1) *sub-divisions* (e.g. rich/middle/poor peasant, discussed below); (2) *intermediate groups* (e.g. rich peasants or 'Kulaks', on the ascent to becoming capitalist farmers: an example which also illustrates *motion*) and (3) *mixed forms*, often much more confusing in rural than in urban areas due to the incomplete nature of proletarianization. Gunder Frank (1969a, pp. 271–2) has put this well, referring to the likelihood of: 'a single worker who is simultaneously (i) *owner* of his own land and house, (ii) *sharecropper* on another's land . . . , (iii) *tenant* on a third's land, (iv) *wage worker* during harvest time on one of these lands, and (v) independent *trader* of his own home produced commodities.' (emphases added.) To 'his', one should add 'hers': for women are fully involved here too, and once you start considering *household* strategies the picture becomes yet more tangled – with wives and husbands, daughters and sons all often doing different things, not infrequently in different places.

However, unlike the bourgeois/proletarian relation (at least in its Marxist form), to speak of a landlord/peasant relation does not necessarily imply any particular theory of exploitation. There can be several types of linkages. We can consider them (like many social phenomena) under three headings, separable conceptually but empirically linked: economic, political and cultural.

There is bound to be an *economic* relation of some kind. In Marxist terms, surplus can be transferred in a variety of ways, typically *not* full wage labour (else we should speak not of peasants, but of farm labourers). These include *sharecropping*, giving up a share of the crop to the landlord (on whose land it has probably been grown); and/or various forms of unpaid *labour service* of a 'feudal' nature. Marx of course speaks of a 'feudal' mode of production, but not a peasant one; hence some Marxists criticize the term 'peasant' as being loose, unscientific, and merely descriptive.

At all events, the lord/peasant relation is typically not economic alone. *Politically*, Marxists stress the non-economic coercion inherent in feudalism. *Culturally*, this is often viewed (by all concerned) as a system of mutual dependence, with rights and responsibilities on both sides; even if to the outsider it looks profoundly unequal. More generally, those who claim that there *is* an entity called peasants who do have something in common often locate that something in the cultural realm. Peasant culture is characterized as wary, fatalistic, deferential, and having a particular view of the 'order of things'.

Yet the 'vertical' links discussed hitherto may not exhaust the topic. In large parts of contemporary Africa, for instance, one might want to use the term 'peasants' even in contexts where no 'feudal' or other landlord class – least of all a traditional one – is necessarily in evidence. A century ago, however, 'peasant' might not have been the right word to use. In order to see why, let us now examine what I have called the 'horizontal' dimension of peasantry. This aspect has been summarized by Kroeber and Redfield, who define peasants as 'a part society with part culture' (quoted in Shanin, 1971, p. 245). And Redfield adds: 'there is no peasantry before the first city' (*ibid* p. 255).

Like the 'vertical', such horizontal linkages to a wider world can be seen as having economic, political and cultural dimensions. *Economically*, peasants are likely to be involved at least to some degree in *markets*, and producing for markets, whether they sell directly or deal through merchants or middlemen. In *politics*, too, there may be middlemen; indeed, it is a classic theme of the political sociology of the Third World how often politics takes a 'clientelist' or 'brokerage' form – a fact usually attributed to peasants' political tendencies. More broadly, peasants are at least in some sense members of (albeit often substantially excluded from participating in) a wider political order, i.e. an empire or nation-state. If nothing else, they are liable to be drafted into the military: most Third World armies are largely composed of peasant conscripts. *Culturally*, according to Redfield (cited in Shanin, 1971, p. 337 ff), peasants have a folk culture or 'Little Tradition' which stands in contrast to (although historically in some instances it is transformed into) the kind of 'Great Tradition' typical of city civilization.

Peasantization

After this necessary detour, you can probably see why the term 'peasant' might *not* have been applicable a century ago to large swathes of Africa, where not only vertical but also these kinds of horizontal linkages scarcely yet existed. Ken Post (1977) has usefully formalized the distinctions between traditional or tribal 'communal cultivators', and the peasants whom they gradually become. *Land ownership* is originally communal (although its *use* may be individual), but becomes individual; indeed, the notion of *ownership* may appear for the first time. Both the social *division of labour*, and *political* hierarchy and obligations, are inseparable from kinship; but with 'peasantization' they each become increasingly autonomous spheres. *Markets* were absent or peripheral, but become increasingly central. And *culture*, once largely homogenous, becomes separated into Redfield's 'great' and 'little traditions'.

Note that Post's contrasting ideal-types represent an actual historical process, which he calls '*peasantization*'. The word is both ugly and surprising yet the idea is essential. We perhaps tend to think of peasants as the ones who were always there in the first place, and whom history tends to bundle more or less unceremoniously off the historical stage as modernization and industrialization take hold. Such an approach may do for Europe, but for much of the Third World (especially Africa) the *creation* of peasantries is a relatively recent and even continuing process. Moreover, in a contradictory compression of what in Europe were separate and successive process, peasantization and proletarianization may be taking place side by side. Palmer and Parsons (1977, p. 2) put this point well, in summarizing the pioneering contribution of Giovanni Arrighi's (1967) work on Rhodesia (now Zimbabwe): 'Arrighi brought out the historical contradictions inherent in capitalist development, first stimulating the growth of a peasantry to supply its food-stuffs, and then proceeding to break up that peasantry in order to obtain its labour'.

Proper Peasants?

Drawing some of the threads together, Shanin (1971, pp. 14–15) suggests a four-part 'ideal type' of peasants. The *family farm* is the basic unit of socialization, involving just about everything: labour, consumption, property, socialization, sociability, and welfare. Secondly, *land husbandry* is the major means of livelihood, directly providing for most consumption needs, at a low level of specialization and technology. Then there is the specific *culture* of small rural communities, stressing tradition and conformism. Finally, there is the peasantry as *underdog*, dominated by outsiders: yet whose linked economic, political and cultural subordination does not prevent them sometimes turning into 'the revolutionary proletariat of our times' (p. 15).

Not everyone would agree with this characterization. In general, Weber's 'ideal type' approach (of which the above is a good example) does not command universal assent. More specifically, Marxists who emphasize relations of production as basic would find more differences than commonality in all of the above. In particular, they would direct attention to the specific relations of particular groups of producers with emerging capitalism; and would probably predict growing class differentiation and polarization among 'peasants', thus eroding whatever homogeneity may once have existed.

Shanin himself insists that 'like every social entity, peasantry exists only as a process, i.e. in its change' (1971, p. 17). What is at issue, though, is what the processes are. The major controversy surrounds the first of Shanin's four points, namely the nature of the *family farm* and its dynamics. Shanin, following the Russian 'populist' agronomist Chayanov (cf. Shanin, 1971, pp. 150–9), regards peasant economy as a distinct type with its own logic, which for complicated reasons has no necessary inbuilt tendency to polarize into separate capitalist classes. This view was opposed in theory by Lenin and in practice by Stalin, with his brutally enforced collectivization of the Soviet peasantry.

While there is probably no single general answer to this question, my own sympathies are more with Shanin. An over-economistic Marxism tends to neglect cultural variables (e.g. the persistence of kinship ties) in its analysis; while in practice it is too hasty in finding 'classes', presuming their interests to be mortally opposed (e.g. rich 'versus' poor peasants), and taking action accordingly. As a result, communist regimes – even those whose revolutions were largely won with peasant support, ironically and tragically – have often pursued wrongheaded or harsh policies with a detrimental effect on both peasant economic output and political support.

Nonetheless, capitalist development in the long run is likely to erode the peasantry. Just how long that run can be, however, is illustrated by France, whose peasantry remains numerous and politically vocal – although it may be a moot point whether family farms possessing tractors, combines, and colour TV are still strictly 'peasant'.

Peasants and Politics

One major controversy over peasants concerns their politics, about which there exist diametrically opposed views. Some (including Marx) saw them as inherently conservative because of their conditions of life, which put caution at a premium and discouraged collective action. Yet, as Eric Wolf (in Shanin, 1971, p. 264) points out, 'six major social and political upheavals, fought with peasant support, have shaken the world of the twentieth century' – in Mexico, Russia, China, Vietnam, Algeria, and Cuba. Indeed, it looks at first sight as if peasants have been doing what Marx thought was the proletariat's job.

Although the issues are complex and each case is different, Wolf suggests that normal peasant passivity has in this century been challenged by three crises: demographic, ecological, and 'power and authority'. Importantly, peasants often see themselves as acting in self-defence, standing up for an old order against the encroachments of (e.g.) large-scale commercial agriculture. John Womack (1972), in his book on Zapata and Mexico, captures this aspect brilliantly. His book begins (p. 14): 'This is a book about country people who did not want to move and therefore got into a revolution. They did not figure on so odd a fate'.

Wolf makes the further point that the key force in such processes is neither the richer peasants who usually have a stake in the status quo, nor the poorest who lack land and hence tactical power, but the 'middle' peasants. It is they who may have both the reasons and resources to resist, and hence find themselves (albeit usually with outside support) making a revolution.

The 'Green Revolution'

In a number of Third World countries, especially in Asia and Latin America, increased crop yields made possible by scientific breakthroughs have brought about dramatic changes in agriculture. There are in fact two good reasons for scrutinizing this 'Green Revolution' (as it has come to be known) in a sociological text: not only for its empirical importance, but also because it provides an object lesson in the interrelation between technical and social factors.

Byres and Crow (1983) have studied the Green Revolution in India, and I largely draw on their account in what follows. As they say (p. 6), ' "Green Revolution" is a slogan which adhered retrospectively to a particular technocratic approach to agrarian change'. What does this imply? In principle, there are a number of ways of boosting agricultural production: increasing crop yields, extending acreage, or having more crops per year. And any of these could in principle be approached in different ways. One could alter the *technical* conditions of production: either *biochemically* (improved strains of seed, fertilizer, pesticide, etc.), or *mechanically* (more machinery, e.g. tractors and combines). Alternatively, and perhaps less obviously, changing the *social* conditions of production may also bring about increased production: paying farmers more for their crop, giving security of tenure, or redistributing land to the landless.

So it is a complex picture, in which there are both interrelations and choices. To dramatize the choice somewhat, the Green Revolution may be seen by governments as the only alternative to a red one. In situations where land shortages and rural inequalities not only caused discontent but placed limits on increasing food production for city and country alike, technical breakthroughs in developing high yielding varieties of grains such as wheat and rice came as something of a godsend, potentially staving off food crises and social unrest – and avoiding the need for any serious and systematic land reform.

However, this 'technical' solution has not in practice proved to be socially neutral. Abundant research evidence shows that the full benefit of high yielding varieties (HYVs) only goes to those well placed to take advantage of them. Without going into all the details, the key link here is in a broad sense 'mechanical'. HYVs need irrigation, which means tubewells, which cost money. The time constraints of multiple cropping favour those who can afford to mechanize harvesting. And, at least in India, the whole new technological 'package' was heavily commercialized: seed (formerly saved from last year's crop) must now be purchased, along with the fertilizers and pesticides without which HYVs would hardly thrive.

So who benefits? At one level, the Indian state and nation as a whole. For the Green Revolution has solved or at least staved off India's chronic food crisis: an achievement which, compared with the position twenty years ago, should not be under-estimated. Yet a more detailed scrutiny shows that the gains are in many ways uneven: accruing principally to particular crops, in specific favoured areas, and to some social classes more than others. The Green Revolution is a *wheat* revolutioh (or, in other countries, a rice revolution). It has boosted production of the cash crop sold to cities, but not of the millet and maize which the rural poor themselves eat; and it has elbowed out the lentils and pulses which helped balance rural diets. By region, it is over-whelmingly the well-watered plains of the Punjab which have become the granary for the rest of India. This has two consequences. Not only is rural life not improved for most Indians; but the Punjab's increasing sense of its own advance and importance is undoubtedly one factor in fuelling separatist political demands, the suppression of which led to Mrs. Gandhi's assassination in 1984.

Specific crops and regions aside, the *class* effects of the Green Revolution are particularly interesting. For, although it is a strategy which involved 'betting on the strong', it has not exactly strengthened the status quo. On the contrary, whereas until the 1950s the landlord class was dominant, it is the *rich peasants* who have gained most from the Green Revolution and 'emerged as masters of the Indian country-side' (Byres and Crow, 1983, p. 47). It was they who had both the incentive and the resources – including, importantly, *access* to institutional credit as much as actual pre-existing wealth – to benefit most.

What of the others? The effects are complex, but those less well placed lose out in various ways. Poorer peasants increasingly lease their land to those richer (who can take advantage of economies of scale). Sharecroppers become in fact or in effect wage labourers, as mechanizing landlords now need their labour less than they want back the land that the sharecroppers occupy. There is growing landlessness (albeit slowly, so far); growing proletarianization (albeit incomplete: labour is still often 'attached' via loan-debts and other forms of personal dependence); and, in particular, a big increase in migrant labour (as Hindu migrants from Bihar, say, travel across India to work on Sikh farms in the Punjab; again, a factor not unrelated to recent communal tensions).

In this account I have focussed on the Indian case, following Byres and Crow (1983). Elsewhere, the details might be different. Other interpretations are possible too. In fact, the Green Revolution literature is often rather polarized in predictable ways. Modernization theorists portray it as a more or less unproblematic success story, in which 'science rules OK'; whereas some dependency approaches leave you with the impression that nothing has changed at all, or only for the worse. I hope the above section has shown how and why both these views are inadequate. Change there has certainly been, both economic and social. But, not unusually, it has benefitted different interests unequally. And if, as seems plausible, the long-term effect is increasing inequality in the countryside, one may wonder whether the technical solution afforded by the Green Revolution will for all time stave off demands for revolution of a different hue – or, at least, for some alterations in the social conditions of production as well.

Peasants in Hyden

The Swedish political scientist Goran Hyden (1980) has written a fascinating book to try to explain why Tanzania has had such uneven success in implementing *ujamaa* socialism, increasing agricultural output, or indeed effecting any kind of rural change. In Tanzania, as in much of Africa, the subsistence-oriented 'peasant mode of production' is particularly resilient. The 'economy of affection' (familial and communal ties) still looms large. Moreover, rainfed agriculture and low population density meant there was no pressure for either co-operation or state-sponsored irrigation to develop, as happened in parts of Asia. The result is that output and productivity levels are very low.

Enter the State. According to Hyden (1980, p. 9) 'economic history is largely the story of how to capture the peasants'. Only in Africa has this still not widely happened yet, as peasantries with their own means of production cling to their independence and tenaciously resist the state's efforts to get a handle on them; even, ironically, in an at least arguably well-meaning socialist state like Tanzania, stressing the African co-operative traditions of *ujamaa*.

What ensues is a game of cat and mouse, delightfully illustrated in the successive chapter titles of Hyden's book. Small is powerful; small rebuffs modern and big; big slips on small; small goes into hiding; small the deceitful; small as infiltrator; the pervasiveness of small; is small really beautiful?; why small remains unexplored. The sly strength of peasantries in evading, resisting and when all else fails infiltrating and subverting state institutions and policies is made very clear. (In fact, Hyden remarks, it is easier for the State to control foreign capital, even, than the peasants!)

Theoretically, Hyden draws on both mainstream and Marxist approaches. He portrays capitalist and precapitalist modes of production in an uneasy kind of symbiosis, with the former in some circumstances strengthening the latter rather than undermining it. He sees the principal barriers to increased production as internal; if anything, capitalism has not exploited the Third World enough. And, like modernization theorists, he insists that peasant institutions and values will have to change.

This last point is crucial. For Hyden does *not* say that small is beautiful; in fact he explicitly queries it. Wherever his sympathies lie, the logic of history and development alike dictate that one way or another, sooner or later, states must take their agriculture in hand and turn it into a modern, efficient, productive sector, guaranteeing a surplus to both feed and invest in urban and industrial development – which in turn will benefit agriculture. One may hope that this will be done *with* the peasants, rather than against them; not only on humanitarian grounds, but also realistically because of their considerable ability to sabotage any programmes and policies which they disapprove of. But, one way or another, it must be done.

Transformation or Improvement?

There is widespread agreement that over much of the Third World existing agrarian relations are unsatisfactory, whether from the view-point of economic efficiency ('delivering the goods', in the form of cash crops or food self-reliance) or social justice. There is much less consensus, however, about what can or should be done about this – and by whom.

It is conventional and convenient to distinguish, as Long (1977, p. 144) does, two basic approaches to changing agriculture. The *improvement* approach seeks to work with and within existing systems of peasant production, in order to make them work better. The *transformation* system, by contrast, aims to make a complete break and establish new organizational forms for agriculture. The former can include the provision of various types of inputs and assistance to existing communities, either singly or in 'packages' such as community development programmes. The latter includes a wide range of different kinds of initiative: plantations, state farms, settlement schemes, land redistribution and reform, or revolutionary measures such as the Chinese commune.

As may be readily seen, 'transformation' in this sense is not only varied but has been going on in the Third World for quite some time already. Long (1977, p. 144) describes it as involving 'a radical break with existing peasant systems in terms of scale of operation, production techniques, and socio-legal structure'. Each of those three points would apply to a capitalist plantation producing sisal in colonial Tanganyika, for instance, as much as to a collective farm in the USSR. So we should be careful to distinguish these three dimensions of *scale, technology,* and *ownership* when trying to assess the arguments for and against the two approaches.

Critics of peasant agriculture suggest that it is inherently unsuited for adaptation to the needs of a modern state. Being principally concerned with subsistence and self-sufficiency, peasants lack the incentive or initiative either to adopt modern technology, or to expand their operations up to a level where they can begin to reap economies of scale. One reason for this is that they tend to see land as more than just a commodity to be bought and sold, and indeed their whole way of life as more than just a question of production inputs and outputs. This sentimental peasant attachment to old ways puzzles and exasperates their critics, who are, however, themselves ideologically divided from this point on. Advocates of large-scale *capitalist* farming are content to create a market in land and wait for the normal market processes to take hold. Socialists, however, have often had an additional and to some extent different set of self-imposed worries.

In a sense trusting peasants both more and less than their capitalist critics, socialists like Lenin envisaged capitalism as evolving in agriculture along two routes simultaneously: not only by the formation of big estates (or, in the European case, their *transformation* from semi-feudalism into large-scale modern farming), but also through a process of differentiation within the peasantry itself. For socialists, then, considerations of politics as well as economics enter in; and their fear of peasants is less that economically they will deliver too little than that politically they will be trouble.

Chapter Six

Population

Demography and development form a paradoxical pair. They are obviously connected, yet the nature of the connexions is both unclear and controversial. Sometimes mistakenly regarded as dry-as-dust number-crunching, and certainly demanding statistical and analytical skills, population dynamics are in fact a profoundly sociological topic: impacting as they do upon such areas as health, gender, the state, industrialization, cultural change, and indeed just about everything.

Population is also a highly political and often polarized topic. Extreme positions abound. For the prophets of imminent eco-doom, population is *the* problem: a time-bomb which if not defused and checked will destroy global civilization in a cataclysm of famine, war and general Malthusian catastrophe. Equally robust views are found at the other extreme, where a distinctly odd coalition of forces – Marxists alongside right wing nationalists, the Roman Catholic church along with optimistic scientific rationalists – denies that there is a problem at all. The world can feed far more people than its present population, and we have neither the right nor the need to limit births. Any move to do so is a (depending on your viewpoint) capitalist, racist, atheist or anti-scientific conspiracy.

Not surprisingly, the clash of positions like these tends to generate more heat than light. Yet within both of these two extremes, as well as between them, can be found defensible views concerning population analysis and policy. A case can be made that population growth is now outstripping and hence cancelling out economic advance in the Third World, such that birth control is the crucial precondition for any other effective steps towards development. The most spectacular convert to such a view is undoubtedly China, which since the early 1970s has dramatically switched sides. We shall discuss the Chinese case later.

Equally, however, one can construct a respectable case for the opposite view. Not necessarily that population is no problem; but that, if the West's experience is anything to go by, economic development and a consequent spread of at least the beginnings of affluence must come first, precisely in order to give people an incentive to start limiting their family size. According to this argument, if governments ignore this fact and try to provide family planning in isolation, they are unlikely to succeed – indeed, such measures may well blow up in their faces.

As we shall see, advocates of this view are on surer ground in worrying about the policy and implementation problems than in their reading of the European historical record. But already this discussion has implicitly raised two pairs of analytical distinctions which we should now make explicit, to be borne in mind in the rest of the chapter. One, which should be familiar in general terms, is the relation between *economic* and *cultural* factors, and their respective role in population change. Is it true that, as a former Indian minister put it, 'development is the best contraceptive'? – implying that economic development is a necessary precondition for the birthrate to decline, rather than vice versa? Alternatively, can people's *attitudes* and hence behaviour regarding procreation change even without or before such development?

This has already raised the other pair of distinctions, which concerns the relationship in all this between *individual* (or family) and *state* policies – or, if you like, micro and macro. Can government policy of whatever kind – stick, carrot, or a combination of the two – be effective in changing people's ideas and practices in this field? and if so, how?

Population Facts and Figures

At the time of writing, the total human population of the world is around 4.5 billion. Within a few years of publication, it will pass the 5 billion mark. 6 billion will be reached before the century is out. Nor is it going to stop there. Any stabilization measures will take time to have effect. (If you think about it, population policies only 'bite', not when and because people have fewer children, but when that smaller generation is *itself* grown up and producing fewer children.)

This situation of rapid population growth is both historically new and unevenly distributed. Taking the very long view, for thousands of years before the Neolithic revolution introduced settled agriculture (and hence the increased productivity which could feed more mouths), world population probably remained stable at a tiny fraction of its present level: perhaps 5–10 million. (Hunters and gatherers need a lot of space.) The great agrarian civilizations were more productive, and by the time BC became AD the figure was probably 200–300 million.

It says much for the demographic stability of pre-industrial societies that this figure was still much the same a thousand years later; thanks to the characteristic combination of high birth *and* death rates, plus periodic crises – famines, plagues, etc. – which meant that in those days populations could fall as well as rise. Things began to pick up again in the early modern period: 400–500 million in 1500, and 550 million by 1650 (though still giving a global rate of increase of no more than a million a year).

Only in the last 200 years has the picture changed out of all recognition, such that growth (and increasingly rapid growth) has become the norm. This timing suggests that, just as the first big spurt coincided with the agrarian revolution, so today's 'population explosion' is connected with industrialization. As we shall see, however, the exact causal relations are not so straightforward as might be supposed. Be that as it may, the numbers are not in doubt (and in modern times, of course, our ability to measure them exactly has been greatly enhanced thanks to national censuses). The billion mark was reached around 1830. It took a century to double to 2 billion (1930), but only thirty years to add the next billion (1960) and sixteen years the one after that (1976). Put another way, 'doubling time' from 2 to 4 billion took 46 years, less than half the previous doubling time.

Population Distribution

The world's population is not evenly distributed, either by absolute number or in terms of *density* (relative to land area). About two-thirds of humankind live in the Third World. Of these, some three quarters (close to 2.5 billion) are in Asia, which thus contains over half the world's population. Even this figure is overwhelmingly accounted for by the world's two mega-nations, China and India, with populations currently of the order of 1000 and 700 million respectively. (These two countries' particular population problems and policies form the subject of a separate section.)

Overall, Asia has a density of some 95 persons per square kilometre (ppkm^2). Coincidentally, Europe's density figure for its half a billion people is almost exactly the same. But the other two major Third World continents, Africa and Latin America, present a very different profile. With populations around 500 and 400 million respectively, their *densities* are in both cases less than 20 ppkm^2 – i.e. only a fifth of the figure for Asia or Europe. This figure should serve as a caution against any naïve view that the *entire* Third World – and *only* the Third World – is densely populated.

Admittedly, population density figures must (like all figures) be interpreted carefully. Like any average, figures for continents conceal a wide range of national and regional variation. Qualitatively too, density per land area alone tells us nothing about the *nature* of the land: whether it is mountains, desert, or fertile soil; whether it has mineral resources; and whether in either case it has a society and level of technology well able to use these resources to sustain a large population.

Also, of course, 'snapshot' density figures in themselves do not reveal the crucial factor, *rate* of growth. Looking at this, we find that it is in fact Africa and Latin America which have the highest rates of natural increase. In 1975–77 these were 2.8% and 2.6% per year respectively, and the African figure was still rising. The figure in Asia was 2.3%; while Europe's was a mere 0.7%. Yet, just twenty years earlier during 1950–55 the European rate had been almost twice as high, at 1.3%. What factors then account for changes in rates of natural increase? And what kinds of policy intervention are appropriate or feasible?

Demographic Transition and the European Experience

Demographic change is a function of three variables: births, deaths, and migration. (You could say: movement into and out of the planet, and movement into or out of particular countries.) In practice, although migration in particular places and times can be very important, it is births and deaths – and particularly the former – which have received most attention.

Reviewing the experience of Europe, a number of writers (including Blacker, Davis, Notestein and Thompson) have detected a particular pattern of 'demographic transition'. Some describe it as having three stages, others four. In either case, the starting and end points are agreed: these are situations of relative population stability, but with very different causes. At the outset, traditional societies are characterized by high fertility *and* high mortality. Blacker calls this the 'high stationary' stage. From society's point of view, the high birth rate cancels out the high death rate. From the individual's point of view, it is necessary to produce a large number of children in order to ensure that at least some survive into adulthood.

In contrast, the final or at least modern stability (for Blacker, 'low stationary') is a result of *low* rates of both birth and death. Now improved living standards and medical advances have dramatically reduced death rates in industrial societies. Since virtually all children born can now be expected to live into adulthood, people no longer need to have so many of them. Affluence too, it is argued, provides a further incentive for having fewer children. People want material possessions and children are a very costly investment. And, of course, a range of effective contraceptive technologies are now available and widely distributed. In some industrial societies (particularly in Eastern Europe, which is interesting), birth rates have now fallen to or even below the point where existing numbers are maintained; in other words, zero or even negative population increase.

What about the intervening stage or stages? The point is that death rates begin to fall before birth rates start to follow suit, and it is a moot point really whether you call this two stages or one. (Blacker distinguishes 'early' and 'late' expanding stages: the former with sharply declining deaths while births remain on a plateau, the latter once births have begun to come down whilst the fall in deaths has also levelled off.) Either way, the obvious result of lower death rates while births remain high is a population explosion: that is what happened in much of 19th century Europe, and that is what is happening in the Third World today. It is obviously of more than antiquarian historical interest to know just how and why Europe shifted out of exploding transition into its modern steady state, since any lessons learned may be applicable to the Third World.

One of the most comprehensive and interesting studies of Europe's experience has been carried out by van de Walle and Knodel (cited in Goldthorpe, 1984, p. 33ff). They were particularly concerned to try to isolate the onset of widespread use of contraceptives, as distinct from the pre-existing differences in 'natural fertility' of various communities. What Goldthorpe pithily calls 'stopping behaviour' (indicated by a noticeable decline in married fertility) was found to occur all over Europe around 1900: rarely earlier than 1880 (except in France), or later than 1920.

This discovery is on the face of it bad news for purely socio-economic explanations, since Europe itself at this time exhibited wide diversity. England was highly industrialized and literate, Hungary mainly illiterate and overwhelmingly agrarian – yet fertility decline began in both at around the same time. So it looks as if the cultural diffusion of ideas is more important. But perhaps we should not polarize economic and cultural factors too sharply here. Just as urbanism affects even those who do not themselves live in cities, so one might suggest that the onset of industrialism in Europe set in train complex changes in attitudes, expectations, and behaviour, which sometimes worked themselves out in advance of actual industrialization in any particular place. Cultural change can follow economic change without being its consequence, and may precede it without necessarily being its cause.

Third World Issues: Culture and Economics

That which in Europe is of historical interest assumes great practical urgency in the Third World. Clearly, developing countries are well into the second stage of demographic transition; but how are they going to get home and dry into the final steady state? Already in the Third World, as occurred earlier in Europe, social improvements and medical advances have begun to reduce death rates. Birth rates, however, have not yet (with some exceptions) followed suit.

What then are the factors which affect fertility in the Third World? As you might expect, there is a range of different theories. Moreover, any explanation has to be adequate to explain both overall trends and individual motivations. Hardiman and Midgley (1982) note that here too there are 'cultural' and 'economic' camps. The former may well imply that high fertility is irrational, but persists as a kind of cultural lag (often contained in religious or similar norms) from the time when traditional societies really did need as many births as possible.

But there are difficulties here. Perhaps surprisingly, not many of the world's major religions do in fact frown on birth control; the Roman Catholic church is almost the only one which does. On a different tack, it is interesting that Hardiman and Midgley use the same historical evidence from Eastern Europe as Goldthorpe does to reach an opposite conclusion. For them, the fact that birth rates fell in Bulgaria *before* industrialization shows that cultural factors (in the form of alleged rural traditionalism) are *not* paramount; while for Goldthorpe this proves that socio-economic conditions are no match for the power of ideas (i.e. knowledge of, and preference for, modern contraceptive methods). Perhaps the moral is that we must be very careful, both to distinguish conceptually what we mean by terms like 'cultural' and 'economic', and to analyze empirically how they interact in practice.

The main objection to culturalist explanations of high fertility, however, challenges head-on the basic premise that having many children *is* irrational. According to this view, the logic of *states* (taking the longer, macro view) and of *households* (who must ensure their own survival in the here and now, and who may have no cause to believe that tomorrow will be much different from yesterday) are liable to diverge, perhaps sharply. For peasants in particular, over and above the felt need for many births in order that at least some children will survive (a view in itself still not wholly irrational, despite falling death rates), more children represent both an extra labour input and insurance for old age – factors which may well counter-balance the (relatively brief) period when they are nothing but an additional mouth to feed.

Admittedly this view is sometimes taken to extremes. Perhaps out of a laudable desire to avoid that ethnocentrisism which would dub any puzzling behaviour as 'irrational', some of the more mathematically-minded economists have not only declared that 'children yield utility' but have actually proceeded to try to calculate it, in terms of 'inter-generational wealth flows' and the like. As with parallel attempts to reduce rural-urban migration to mathematical cost-benefit calcula-tions, one suspects this is overdone. As Hardiman and Midgley drily observe, conception is more a matter of emotion than of economics. (To put it another way, it is not usual to make love while holding a pocket calculator.) Nevertheless, a modern classic study like Mamdani's (1972) in the Punjab supports the broad view that poor peasants see children as an economic asset – perhaps their only one. In this instance the villagers were polite enough to accept the contraceptives offered by a high-powered US family planning project, whose experts then puzzled over why the project was having no visible effect: but they simply didn't actually take the tablets!

Finally, Hardiman and Midgley note how some have tried to argue that economic development alone will not cause fertility to fall unless linked with social development, 'basic needs', and similar distributional issues. This hypothesis helps explain some kinks in the statistics, but (like most attempts at a general theory, in this field) fails to iron out others. As ever, there are still counter-instances in both directions; and, as ever, it is not easy to spell out precisely the alleged links in the model's chain.

Population Policies: India and China

It is hardly surprising that the two biggest countries in the Third World and indeed the whole world (both have populations well over twice as large as anywhere else) should be in the forefront of policy measures to control their rates of increase. Although China and India are untypical by the very scale of their problem, and their approaches have been rather different, nonetheless their experiences are interesting and instructive.

India, according to Goldthorpe (1984, p. 37) was the first country in the world whose government actively favoured family planning – from soon after independence in 1947. As successive degrees of encouragement failed to have a noticeable impact, however, with the birthrate remaining over 40 per 1000 in the late 1960s, the stakes got higher. Ironically, Dr. Karan Singh, the very same minister who had coined the slogan 'the best contraceptive is development', now did a U-turn and called for a 'direct assault' on the 'vicious circle' of population growth. His wish was granted, but it got seriously out of hand. There were widespread reports of excessive pressure and even compulsory vasectomies and sterilizations, which played a major part in the late Indira Gandhi's losing the general elections of 1977. She got back in later, of course, and with or without her the family planning programme went on, albeit in a lower key. Yet any progress is slow, not least because even if birth rates do come down death rates are still doing likewise. Thus according to figures quoted by Hardiman and Midgley (1982, p. 70), although India's crude birth rate declined from 43 to 35 per 1000 between 1960 and 1978, a parallel fall in the death rate (from 21 to 14 per 1000) meant that the overall rate of natural increase in 1978 was only fractionally less than it had been almost twenty years earlier: 2.1% as against 2.2%.

By contrast, the equivalent figures for China for the same years are in every respect more dramatic: birth rate halved from 36 to 18, death rate slashed from an already low 15 to an extraordinary 6 (in part a statistical freak, this; though seemingly lower even than in most developed countries, this reflects an age-structure in process of change, in which – so to speak – the first generation that is living longer has not yet begun to die off); and the overall rate of natural increase sharply cut from 2.1% to 1.2%. All this is the more remarkable considering that China was a late starter in these matters, the communist government having been strongly against population control for some twenty years after it took power in 1949.

Then again, China arguably has both organizational and cultural resources (in the form of the Communist Party and the Confucian heritage, respectively) for implementing the edicts of central authority. Nonetheless, China has had its problems too, notably since the introduction of a 'one-child' policy in the late 1970s, backed by a whole range of sticks and carrots: financial inducements for couples who adhere to the policy, withdrawal of certain welfare benefits from those who do not. While it is as yet too early to judge the success or overall results of this policy, certain illuminating and disturbing effects are already becoming apparent.

In general, the form of the policy seems to run counter to the Chinese government's overall attempts to loosen state control, while its content goes against many deeply ingrained cultural assumptions. For one thing, traditional preference for male children has led to statistics in some Chinese provinces showing up an extraordinary preponderance of male births which can only be attributed to a revival of female infanticide. In other words, if you're only allowed one child then it had better be a boy. (However, according to recent reports, rural couples whose firstborn is a girl are allowed another try.) Also, in a society where aged parents are still provided for by their children, it has been calculated that if successful the new policy – coupled with an already changing age structure, as people live longer – would lead to an impossible burden, whereby each working adult of the next generation might eventually be responsible for up to 6 elderly relatives.

Or again, even if the new policy is taking effect in towns (either because social control is easier there, or because urban couples are inclined in any case to have fewer children), it faces an uphill struggle in the countryside. Chinese peasants, like those elsewhere, have both economic and cultural reasons to prefer several children. At all events one seems an impossibly low figure. There is evidence that at any rate the increasing numbers of wealthier peasants are ignoring the new policy and cheerfully paying the economic penalties, secure in the knowledge (or belief) that they can afford to – not least, because an additional child is seen not so much as a mouth to feed but as an extra pair of hands (and, of course, a provider for one's old age: peasants don't get pensions, even in China).

The World Fertility Survey (WFS)

As it happens, possibly the biggest social survey ever is about population in the Third World. Started in 1972 and still being written up, the WFS has involved sampling 42 developing and 20 developed countries, whose population adds up to around 40% of the world's total. In each country several thousand women have been interviewed (nearly all the interviewers are women too), so the total global sample numbers some 340,000. Most of the research was done in the late 1970s, and by the mid 1980s most of the country studies have been published. What do they show?

In the first place, it looks as if in every continent of the Third World bar one fertility has begun to decline, albeit slowly. Women used to have 4–5 children each, twice as many as their First World sisters and twice what is needed simply to replace (i.e. maintain) existing population levels. That figure has now fallen by an average of one child per woman. The exception is Africa, where birth rates continue high; and where one country, Kenya, for no very clear reason has the world's highest rate of increase at around 4% a year.

Awareness of contraceptive devices is also well-nigh universal. Access to and use of them is another question, however. Goldthorpe (1984) reads the evidence as suggesting 'spacing' rather than 'stopping' behaviour. That is, Third World women so far are using contraception to save their health from the risk of too frequent pregnancies, rather than (as in Europe) to ensure that after a given point they have no more children at all.

The WFS has found too a correlation between fertility and certain socio-economic indicators. On the whole, fewer children are born to women with more education, or who live in towns, or who are employed outside the household.

The WFS figures tend to confirm other general surmises. Thus Bogue and Tsui (cited in Goldthorpe, 1984, p. 34) already in 1978 identified five socio-economic factors as correlating with fertility decline. Working from aggregate national rather than individual data, they found the highest rates of decline among those Third World countries which were: richest, most urbanized, most industrialized, best educated; and which had the lowest infant mortality rates. Over and above all these, however, government family planning programmes were found to have an important effect in their own right. On this basis, Bogue and Tsui concluded that by the late 1970s an overall global downturn in fertility had at last begun.

Chapter Seven

Health

Introduction

Commonsense might query what health has to do with sociology anyway; isn't it a matter for expert medical professionals? However, as sociologists are so fond of pointing out, commonsense can be misleading. Not only is the sociology of health and medicine an important and fascinating field in its own right, but in the Third World context the issues which it raises are of great practical urgency and theoretical importance. This chapter will try to show how many health problems in the Third World need to be analyzed as *social* phenomena.

Colonialism and Health

Colonialism affected people's health, directly and indirectly, in a number of ways. A 'modernisation' account would see this as wholly or largely positive: bringing the benefits of modern Western medical techniques to populations previously at the mercy of all kinds of dread tropical diseases which they were unable to cure or prevent.

Although as we shall see there has indeed been progress in such areas as life expectancy and infant mortality, the above view is much too simple. To be brutal, colonialism in its early stages killed millions of people: not only in various acts of genocide, or the massive depredations of the slave trade, but also by introducing hitherto unknown European diseases to Third World populations unable to resist them. However unintentional, the effects were devastating. Far more Indians died of disease resulting from Western conquests and settlement in the Americas and the Caribbean that were killed outright.

Even at a later stage, when rudimentary health services began to be introduced into colonies by now 'pacified', they had serious limitations. The fact that most such services were initially designed to serve only European colonial officials (plus, later, indigenous employees of the administration) had two harmful effects. One was that these services' scale (small) and location (urban) meant that they simply did not reach the vast rural majority. The other, less obvious, was that the Third World thus inherited a *type* of medical care – European-style, curative in intent, patient-centred, and hospital-based – of doubtful relevance to its actual problems and needs. Both these factors remain today as major question marks over the quantity and quality of Third World health provision.

Less directly, but of stark contemporary relevance today, the fact that colonialism often entailed the replacement of growing food for one's own subsistence by cash crop production for foreign markets has been one factor in precipitating a chronic food crisis in many Third World countries. In extreme cases, the result is famine and mass starvation. Less visibly, there is evidence that 'mono-cultivation' (growing a single cash crop) has led to many people's diets becoming less balanced over time. An example which haunts me is from 'socialist' Tanzania, even, in the early 1970s. In an area of protein-deficient diets, people were forbidden to pick cashew nuts from the trees – because they were earmarked for export, to earn foreign exchange.

Traditional Medicine and Healers

All societies, by definition, have had some procedures for dealing with the sick. Many had specialized practitioners in this field, such as herbalists or midwives. In the Third World, however, the colonial impact often led to such knowledge being dismissed wholesale as un-scientific 'mumbo-jumbo', and its practitioners being labelled as 'witch-doctors'. 'Scientific' medicine was equated with modern Western techniques – even while, ironically, these were scarcely available to most people, who largely continued (and still do) to have recourse to traditional remedies, nowadays often in conjunction with Western ones.

It is true that some indigenous practices were unhygienic or even dangerous, and many practitioners probably could not give a 'scientific' account of what they did or why. Nevertheless, the balance of opinion and practice is now changing, in several ways. First, many traditional herbal remedies have been found to work, and chemical analysis can show how and why they work. Second, there are techniques which appear to succeed even though their theoretical basis is not well understood – the best known being Chinese acupuncture. Related to this, even in the West itself there is a decline of exclusive faith in 'established' medicine, coupled with an open-mindedness to alternative traditions (e.g. homeopathy or osteopathy) which the dominant medical profession has tried to marginalize or suppress.

Above all, and good news for sociologists, there is increasing recognition that medical relations are also social relations. Traditional healers undoubtedly had and have important social roles – in their communities generally, and in their relations with individual patients – which contribute to their success and the continuing respect in which they are often held. The coming years may well see greater tolerance and even interaction between traditional and modern medicine, to their mutual benefit – which in turn should enhance the health and well-being of Third World peoples.

Health Data

Data in this field suffer from all the usual pitfalls. Many figures do not exist; some which do exist may not be accurate; and as always there is the question of what figures mean. There can also be statistical freaks: a country with apparently high infant mortality may simply have a better death reporting service. Demographic change also interferes: some Third World countries have lower death-rates than some in the West, simply because the age-structure of their populations is changing.

Nonetheless, certain demographic indicators are widely agreed to provide useful evidence of changing patterns of health. Crude death rates have shown a steady decrease over the last thirty years. More specifically, *infant mortality* is declining, but in a pattern illustrating regional diversity: falling fastest in East Asia, and most slowly elsewhere in Asia and in Africa. Yet overall Third World infant mortality is often still five or six times greater than in the West, and many countries still have rates as high at 100–150 per 1000 (Hardiman and Midgley, 1982).

Life expectancy is another useful indicator. Again there has been steady global progress: in the Third World, the average rose from 32 in 1939 to 49 in 1970 (while in the West it has gone up from 56 to 70). However, like many averages these figures are misleading, and in two ways. First, they do not mean in the Third World – although they may do in the West – that these are the ages at which most people actually die. In many Third World countries 40% of *all* deaths are of children under 5 – compared with under 3% in the North.

Secondly, once again global progress conceals variation by country and region. While several Latin American countries have life expectancies of around 70, comparable to the North, Asian averages are closer to 60 and African figures are around 50 or even lower. All in all, 'life-chances' in the most literal sense still differ greatly on our planet, both as between North and South and within different regions of the South.

Incidence of Disease

Similar differences are evident in patterns of incidence of disease, which are clearly related (amongst other things) to two factors: *diet*, and *age*. Thus the two major causes of death in the North are neoplasms and cardiovascular disorders – in plain English, mostly cancers and heart disease – which are associated not only with older populations but also (it is increasingly argued) with over-rich and fatty diets.

The South's problem is the opposite in both respects. Far and away the biggest killers are communicable diseases: most of them not exotically tropical, but including many infections which were common in the North too within living memory – like tuberculosis or diphtheria – or which are still widespread but regarded as minor, e.g. measles or diarrhoea. It comes as a shock to think of measles or diarrhoea as major killers. Yet children in the Third World are especially vulnerable here; all the more so when (as often) they are already weakened by malnutrition and inadequate diets. In fact the largest single disease-affected group in the Third World is children.

Disease, like most things, is also *gender*-specific in ways which are clearly social. Although under equal conditions women's life expectancy is a few years higher than men's, over much of the Third World this gap is narrowed, and in some cases (notably the Indian subcontinent) it is actually reversed. Factors here include nutrition: in some societies men and male children eat first and get the lion's share, while women and girls (who have probably prepared everyone's food) must make do with what is left. Childbirth is also hazardous: too many pregnancies, too little space between them, insufficient care at all stages (from ante-natal to the delivery itself to post-natal) and poor nutrition all take their toll, separately and in conjunction.

Two other factors of disease incidence are worth mentioning. One is obvious: in the South as in the North, only more starkly so, the *poor* suffer ill-health much more than the rich. The other may be less obvious. Despite the obvious health hazards of Third World urban slums, *rural* populations are even worse off: they have far fewer doctors, they are much further from hospitals and health centres, and are even less likely to have access to clean water or effective sanitation. I mention this, because of a tendency in the North to romanticize especially the alleged virtues of rural poverty in the South, as some sort of natural 'world we have lost'.

Needless to say, all of the above factors also interact, and their cumulative weight can be appalling. Thus the health prospects for female children of the undernourished rural poor may be very grim indeed.

Patterns of Disease

It may be useful to go into some detail on the types of diseases prevalent in the Third World, for three reasons. The first is related to the general issue of *recapitulation*. How far is the South's experience of health and disease repeating the North's history in this field? Secondly, there is the claim of *sociology*. If you're ill, you need a doctor, not a sociologist. Such is the commonsense view. And yet we are entitled to ask how far in the South today, as in the North yesterday, medical problems may have social causes and require political solutions (e.g. environmental and sanitation improvements). Finally, facts are important in themselves – and these facts are particularly striking, even shocking. For the fact is that millions in the Third World still die of communicable diseases which are preventable, yet which are endemic in many areas (especially rural areas), and whose incidence is in some cases actually on the increase. Or, even where not fatal, such diseases can be chronic and debilitating, thus affecting individuals' and indeed whole communities' chances of living and working effectively.

Communicable diseases are grouped according to their *vector*, i.e. what carries them. In most cases, not to mince words, this is shit. Infections transmitted through *human faeces* (often via flies) include:

- *diarrhoeas*: a major killer, especially of young children.
- *bacterial or viral diseases*: including polio (on the increase in some countries), cholera (of which new strains have developed since the 1960s), hepatitis and typhoid.
- *parasitic infections*: including two, ascariasis and hookworm, which infest an estimated 650 and 450 million people respectively.

Partially, excepting this last category, much of the above would have been familiar in nineteenth-century Europe.

A second major category is *air-borne* diseases, which account for up to a third of all deaths in the Third World. These include such familiar names as: tuberculosis, pneumonia, bronchitis, whooping cough, diphtheria, meningitis, and influenza. Their familiarity (as names) is instructive. All these are found in the West, but are treatable hence rarely fatal – although it is not so long since many were killers here too. This category also includes the single total success story to date: smallpox, now eradicated worldwide and existing only in laboratories.

A third category, more specifically tropical, involves *insect* or other animal vectors. The best known is the chronic fever *malaria* (which was once found in England), transmitted by mosquitoes. Half a billion people are still at risk from this disease, although campaigns (of drainage, etc.) have had some effect: three-quarters of malarial areas in 1950 were malaria-free by 1970. But resistance, both to insecticides (e.g. DDT) and medications, is a growing problem. Other diseases in this category include schistosomiasis (bilharzia), carried by a water snail, which debilitates some 200 million people; trypanosomiasis (sleeping sickness), which affects 30 to 40 million people and is usually fatal; filarial parasites, including elephantiasis, with 250 million sufferers; and onchocerciasis (river blindness).

Still a fourth group of diseases travel by *contact*, including leprosy, yaws, and VD. They affect relatively fewer but still very many people; perhaps 10–15 million for leprosy, and 40 million for yaws. As for VD, global incidence of syphilis and gonorrhea in the late 1960s was over 50 million and 160 million respectively. Now there is AIDS too, which at least in its Third World manifestations (in Central Africa, so far) has no particular connection with homosexuality. And this category or the previous (scientists are not sure) will include *trachoma*, which affects no fewer than 600 million people and is the major cause of blindness in the world (Hardiman and Midgley, 1982).

I have deliberately given a lot of detail above, because I trust you find these facts as appalling as I do. In most cases (not all, admittedly), millions of people – especially small children – are still dying of perfectly preventable diseases. We know, from the West's experience, how to prevent or at least severely check the worst effects of many of the major communicable diseases. Moreover, we know that the necessary measures are not usually on the frontiers of medical technology (expensive 'wonder-drugs' and the like), but would involve relatively cheap and simple actions such as immunization. In some countries, hearteningly, action on immunization is beginning to be taken. Brazil in 1984 had a massively promoted national campaign aiming to reach every child. And even in strife-torn El Salvador, in early 1985, a day's truce was declared in the civil war so that a mass vaccination programme for children could be carried out.

Yet although such medical programmes are vital, our own history teaches us that the crucial first steps are not medical at all, but social.

Health and Social Factors

Not only were many of the diseases outlined above familiar in the West in the 19th century; but the crucial fact is that in most cases their incidence had fallen dramatically by the early 20th century, *before* their defeat was consolidated by the discovery of antibiotics and vaccines. One way or another, therefore, the fall in disease was connected with improvements in living standards: improved diets, less crowded housing, more education, cleaner water, better sanitation, disposal of wastes, and the like. Although all the precise connections are not fully understood or agreed, the general correlation is pretty clear.

An awful lot of it boils down (as you might say) to *water*. Indeed, some estimates suggest that as much as 80% of all Third World disease is water-related. The connections are clear from the account given above. Yet few people in the Third World, urban or rural, have access to an adequate quantity or quality (and both aspects are crucial) of water. Piped water supplies are still far from the norm, especially in rural areas. Even where they do exist, they may be polluted. Where there is no piped supply, as in most rural areas, water must be fetched. Water is heavy to carry: yet carried it is, almost invariably by women and children, often on their heads over long distances. Not surprisingly, water so obtained is little and precious, such that to use it for washing may well seem a luxury.

Water is also a major factor in *sanitation*. Most of the Third World, urban or rural, still lacks adequate and effective sewage disposal systems. Yet, for as long as this lack continues, faecally-transmitted diseases will continue to infest and kill millions of people – just as they did in the dank cities of early-industrializing Europe, a century and more ago. *Overcrowding* is another social factor contributing to ill-health: not only through high-density urban slums and consequent infection, but equally in 'under-populated' rural areas where many may share one room and eat from a single pot.

Health Policies

Conditions like those described above cry out for action. Yet effective health policies in the Third World are hampered by tradition. Not, for once, 'tradition' in the modernization theorists' sense, meaning backward cultural practices (although to be sure these do play a part), but in this case the tradition is the Third World's colonial inheritance.

Colonialism fostered a lop-sided health care system. I described it above as 'curative . . . patient-centred, and hospital-based', and it is now time to go into this in more detail.

Preventive/curative is one of the most basic distinctions in the sociology of health. They are not, of course, in principle opposed: a good health system will include both prevention and cure. Nor is it universally the case that prevention is cheap while cures are costly. Yet overall it is increasingly now agreed that Third World health care has put the cart before the horse. Far too many resources have gone into building, maintaining and staffing costly Western-style hospitals at the expense of all other health priorities. Despite their vast cost, these hospitals still mostly reach only the privileged and city-dwellers. Even more seriously, this system only intervenes once patients are already ill. It does little or nothing to prevent them *becoming* ill, a task which would entail very different priorities: public health campaigns, mass immunization, adult education (e.g. about balanced diets or personal hygiene); draining swamps, building latrines, providing clean piped water, and generally mobilizing people to participate in improving their own health, not only as individual 'patients' but also as whole communities.

In the West, on the whole, the development of preventive and curative medicine went hand in hand. If anything, 'social' public health measures often *preceded* strictly 'scientific' improvements in medicine itself, e.g. antibiotics. Moreover, many public health measures are relatively cheap. It would only cost $1 million – chickenfeed, for a government – to provide basic immunization for every single child in Peru. Even those measures involving public works can be inexpensive if communities are mobilized, e.g. to build their own latrines. Indeed, some economists would argue that this kind of expenditure isn't even a cost or a drain on resources at all, but an investment. After all, a healthy population constitutes 'human capital' for development; conversely, people who are disease-ridden and under-nourished cannot work very productively in industry or agriculture.

Why then is more not being done? And why does so much that is wrong continue to be done? Part of the answer is sheer 'systems inertia'. A given structure has been inherited, and will continue until and unless enough people are motivated to seek to change it. But there are also vested interests involved in at least three ways. One is the clientele. Existing curative hospital-based medical systems serve and suit the wealthier urban classes pretty well. After all, *their* living conditions (unlike those of the majority of their compatriots) are already such as to ensure few problems on the preventative/public health side.

A second group with an interest in the status quo are Western TNCs, who supply almost all the equipment and above all the drugs to Third World hospitals. These are dealt with in a separate section. The third and perhaps the most important group also deserves a section to itself: the medical profession.

TNCs and Health

The role of TNCs in relation to health has been particularly controversial in recent years. By their own lights, they would probably see themselves as providing to the Third World the advantages of up-to-date drugs, or such modern conveniences as powdered milk for infants. Argument rages, however, on the way TNCs set about this.

The fact that (as we have seen) the Third World's major priority ought to be prevention rather than cure is not in itself the TNCs' fault. They can hardly be blamed for seeking to supply a market whose value has been estimated at $20 billion annually. The question is how they go about it. Several studies have lent weight to numerous Third World complaints, which include the following:

1) The drug companies – which are very few, very big, and of course all based in the First World – use their monopoly power to maintain high prices for an artificially wide range of 'brand name' drugs, in cases where the basic 'generic' drug could in fact be supplied much more cheaply. Since even the Conservative government in Britain is currently in conflict with the drug companies on this issue, one can imagine how weaker Third World governments fare.

2) Particular drugs which may be dangerous are nonetheless sold in the Third World. This may include pre-testing, before a product is deemed safe for the West; or dumping of drugs now banned in the West, e.g. because of harmful side-effects. Most often, it involves drugs which in the West would be prescription-only being sold freely over the counter, often with inadequate instructions and warnings.

3) Very little drug research and development is done in the Third World, or for that matter on Third World diseases.

Of course, in principle it is up to Third World governments to act to prevent abuses like these: e.g. by legislation; by setting up their own basic pharmaceutical industries; or by sticking to the World Health Organisation's list of 200 basic generic drugs. But the drug TNCs still exercise considerable power – not least, as a crucial part of the entire inappropriate individual and curative-based system, whose few actual

Third World beneficiaries are precisely the urban elites who sustain and indeed mostly constitute the governments in question. (This is a good illustration of how wrong it is to counterpose 'external' *versus* 'internal' causes of underdevelopment; for a case like the above precisely shows how 'external' dependency becomes internalized and takes root within the actual structures of Third World societies.)

The issue of powdered baby milk illustrates a similar point, in a slightly different way. Here, although in principle it is surely progress for women to have the option of bottle-feeding if they so choose, the concrete issue concerns the way in which TNCs set out through powerful advertising campaigns to create the impression that bottle-feeding was the only 'modern' method. Since Western cultural aspirations are more widely internalized than the means to fulfil them, the consequence was that (especially in Africa) women went in for bottle-feeding who could not afford it. As a result, either through over-dilution or unsterilized bottles or both, very many babies have suffered malnutrition and death who could have fed much more healthily from their mothers' breasts. Worst of all, even though this issue has generated considerable publicity, it is not clear that all the TNCs concerned have yet stopped pushing their product in the Third World.

The Medical Profession in the Third World

Just as there is no reason why health care provision should take any particular organizational form, the same applies to health personnel. In particular, one may well feel that there is no obvious logical rationale why workers in this field should be so starkly divided between a small highly trained and generously paid elite (mostly male) on the one hand, and a much larger group (mostly female) whose skills receive less formal accreditation and who therefore receive much lower pay and status.

Like the West, the Third World has doctors and nurses too (although the latter are not always so predominantly female). It may seem a harsh judgement, but in many ways doctors seem as much part of the problem as of any solution. Their whole training fits them for curative medicine, and to defend a curative-based system – or indeed to extend it, as general hospitals acquire even more expensive specialist units, and medical schools expand into ever-costlier areas of post-graduate expertise in order to train a handful of students. (In Peru, to train a single doctor costs six thousand times more than to educate a peasant child.) In most countries, doctors have lucrative private practices, as well as or instead of – but in either case at the expense of – any state or public post. (As a general aside, it is not widely realized in the West that most people in the Third World *pay* directly, in one way or another, for any medical care they receive: doctors' bills, medications, etc. Ironically, it is only in some rich Northern countries that medical care is free, not in the poor South.)

Nor is this all. As Hardiman and Midgley put it (1982, p. 170), these doctors 'are trained to treat the diseases of the urban rich rather than ... of the rural poor'. Figures for number of doctors per patient, already predictably low for much of the Third World in any case, are positively appalling when broken down by urban and rural areas. In Kenya, in 1975, the rural ratio was an astonishing *62 times* higher than the urban one (*ibid.* p. 171).

And not only do Third World doctors not like working in rural areas; many choose not to use their skills in and for the Third World at all. The so-called 'brain-drain' of professionals from South to North especially affects doctors. Of some 60,000 foreign doctors in the USA, the majority are of Third World origin. And the British National Health Service relies heavily on doctors from the Indian sub-continent, who are therefore no longer available to work in their countries of origin.

The point here is not to be judgmental about individuals or even social groups, but rather to note that as a *system* none of this does much to promote better health in the Third World. What then can be done instead?

Healthy Socialism

Fortunately, there is evidence that there are alternatives and that they do work. Such evidence comes mainly from two rather different sources. One, as already mentioned, is the experience of the now developed Northern countries (West and East) in public health and preventative medicine. The other is that minority of Third World countries which (in some cases while remaining quite poor) have pursued a socialist development strategy. This does not necessarily entail revolution. Examples include China, Cuba, Vietnam and now Nicaragua, but also cases of social democracy like Costa Rica and Sri Lanka.

What all these, and some others, have in common is simply that their governments have in various ways given priority to preventive medicine and primary health care. As we have seen above, what needs to be done is not really very technically controversial, complicated, or even expensive. But most Third World governments lack the organizational means or the political will to implement change.

Probably the best known area of innovation involves so-called 'barefoot doctors'; or, more exactly, medical auxiliaries. Such terms in fact can cover a considerable range of ideas, roles, and practices in different countries, all of which share the aim of bridging the gaps between doctor/nurse and doctor/patient by creating intermediate personnel. Often, such a role will be at least in part preventative: working out of a local community and promoting immunization and public health measures, as well as dealing with minor ailments in local health centres while referring more serious cases onward to a doctor and perhaps ultimately thence to hospital (for both of these, despite all that has been said above, obviously still have a crucial place in a balanced system of health care provision).

Conclusion

Historically, indigenous Third World health practices were largely suppressed, superseded or marginalized by colonial health systems, which in turn have shaped health provision today. *Culturally*, indigenous beliefs and practices (which in some cases no doubt were and are indeed unhealthy, unscientific, or both) have been widely blamed or denigrated. Yet, ironically, a no less irrational acquired cultural attachment to the idea of 'West is Best' has if anything done even more damage, or at least failed to fulfil its promise of betterment.

Socially, systems of health provision often grossly unequal (in their impact on town and country, rich and poor, men and women) are tenaciously defended by the few who benefit from them and the even fewer professionals who staff them. *Politically*, this pressure is hardly if at all resisted by governments who either share these priorities, or lack the political will or means to confront and change them – especially if this entails the difficult and dangerous task of in some degree actively mobilizing dispossessed groups and communities. *Economically*, it is almost the worst of all possible worlds. Governments grudgingly devote relatively small proportions of their budgets to financing costly, inappropriate and expensive systems of health care which reach hardly anybody – and the no less costly medical schools which preserve them. Conversely, cheap preventative public health measures are neglected; and health expenditure as investment in 'human capital' is scarcely considered.

What then of modernisation *versus* dependency theory? As always, there is no single or uniform answer; and nor do these two approaches necessarily cover or exhaust all the important or interesting issues in any particular field. My own view is probably clear enough from the foregoing discussion: the Third World's lop-sided, 'cart before horse' acquisition of Western-style curative medicine without its preventative complement is a rather good example of the sort of thing dependency theory is on about.

There is no need or call for exaggeration here. It is unnecessary, and in my judgment false, to claim that over most of the world health conditions were *better* before the coming of Western medicine. The onward march of such statistics as rising life expectancy and falling infant mortality testifies to global progress, albeit still too slowly and unevenly. From this, the broad picture, modernization theory might draw some comfort; as also from the point about *recapitulation* stressed earlier, that many of the public health problems and diseases that the Third World faces today were much the same in 19th century Europe.

But such similarity of *problem* is surely outweighed by the acute differences in the *solutions* adopted, and their effectiveness (or lack of it). As so often, the way in which the Third World acquired the potential benefits of Western 'progress' – partial, uneven, and perverse – has largely worked so far to limit its impact and prevent its promise from being fully realized. How long those affected will tolerate this is another question.

Chapter Eight

Education

Introduction

Every human society has always had some form of education; if by this we mean the passing on from generation to generation of such knowledge, skills and values as the group in question possesses and prizes. It has been the distinctive contribution of modern industrial societies to *formalize* this process: that is, to have it done in specific places (schools), by specific personnel (teachers), to age-specific groups (children and young adults), and in a specific way (book-learning).

For modernization theory, as you might expect, modern education is a good thing. If anything that is an understatement. Education is seen as *the* major means of accomplishing modernization, at both societal and individual levels. From the viewpoint of governments, education has a threefold value. *Economically*, it provides the trained 'human capital' (at a price, to be sure; but this is an investment) which will 'staff' development and hence enhance it at every level: efficient administrators, knowledgeable entrepreneurs, literate clerks, skilled workers, scientifically aware peasants. *Politically*, it helps the vital task of nation-building by welding a nation out of what may well be diverse ethnic groups and tribes: an important task of political socialization, as indeed of social control. *Culturally*, likewise, it frees people from ignorance, superstition and backwardness, creating a modern consciousness and community.

Such goals and aspirations are mirrored at the level of the individual too. For an early modernization theorist like Lerner, education (especially literacy, and alongside other factors like urbanization and exposure to mass media) plays a crucial role in producing modern 'mobile personalities', characterized by rationality and 'empathy' (the ability to put yourself in other people's shoes). Similarly, Inkeles and Smith's large-scale survey of some 6000 men in six Third World countries in the mid 1960s found education to be the most important single factor in producing 'individual modernity', which they summarized as involving informed participation, personal efficiency, individual autonomy, and open-mindedness (quoted in Goldthorpe, 1984, p. 241). And certainly education is almost universally seen in the Third World as the only way to get on: to escape from agriculture, get a white-collar job, make something of yourself.

Dependency theory, not unexpectedly, casts a distinctly critical eye over most of this. Some of its criticisms overlap with the more general radical critique of education within the Western sociological debate, while others are specific to the Third World context. While there is no general hostility to modern education systems as such (except for the rather different argument of Illich, which we discuss below), there is much querying of the particular form it has taken, its priorities, implications and effects.

Using the same three headings as above: *economically*, existing education systems are criticized as top-heavy, spending too much on secondary and tertiary provision for a small elite at the expense of primary education for the masses. But this is not surprising, since *politically* the colonial origins of Third World education systems were designed precisely to foster and bolster an indigenous elite, first as auxiliaries to the colonial power and now (since independence) as a ruling class still subordinate to neo-colonial metropolitan power and influence.

No small part of that influence is *cultural*. For a distinctive and tragic result of modern education in the Third World, on this view, is a specifically *cultural dependence*; what Frantz Fanon, the revolutionary French-Caribbean psychiatrist who fought with the Algerian independence movement, called a 'colonized personality'. In total contrast to the almost lyrical view of someone like Lerner, in which the modern personality is seen as some sort of liberated free spirit, the cultural dependency approach paints a sad picture of an isolated and rootless elite infected by individualism, over-identifying with the West, hence ignorant and scornful of (or in any case cut off from) their own societies. In some cases, they may not even speak 'their own' language, but only (or primarily) English or French.

In sum, where modernization theory sees beneficial *diffusion* of Western institutions or cultural values, critics see the creation of harmful *dependence*.

Indigenous Education and Colonialism

Prior to the introduction of modern education, different societies in what is now the Third World had a great variety of education and socialization systems. On the one hand, China had had centuries of entry to the governing bureaucracy by a stiff formal examination. At the other extreme, small-scale preliterate societies (e.g. in Africa) might have had nothing we could recognize as schools at all. Nonetheless, various socialization processes took place, such as initiations and the learning of practical skills, often under the direction of many adults, sometimes in specific places, at particular ages, in groups usually segregated by sex. (You may recall Kunta Kinte in such a scene, in the first episode of *Roots*.)

Elsewhere, there were surplus-producing societies (producing a surplus over and above subsistence) which had a state machinery and written languages. These usually had some form of schooling, often under religious control (e.g. Islamic societies). The coming of colonialism continued the link between education and religion in a new way, inasmuch as it was often Christian missionaries rather than the colonial state as such which first set up Western-style schools. In colonies of mixed religious affiliation, such as Nigeria, this produced an ironic result. The relatively more developed Muslim northern societies did not want Christian missions, which as a result were largely confined to the then less developed smaller-scale animist societies of the south. As a result, the South educationally 'overtook' the North, and there was created a preponderance of better-educated southerners in late-colonial and post-independence Nigeria: a fact which contributed to the rivalries and mutual suspicion which in the mid-60s produced the Biafra war.

Educational Data and Trends

Hardiman and Midgley (1982) provide a useful global progress report. As ever, the data (where available) may be suspect. School enrolment ratios and claimed literacy percentages are especially likely to be inflated, e.g. by ignoring absenteeism and drop-out rates – the latter often very high in the Third World.

Nonetheless, taking a broad sweep over the last thirty years, the picture that emerges is one of broad advance – but unevenly so, and lately with worrying signs of deceleration. In the period 1950–1965, *primary* school enrolments worldwide increased by 95 million. Yet a UNESCO projection for 1970–1985 suggests that, although *percentage* enrolments are still going up, this has now slowed to a rate such that absolute *numbers* of children *not* in school are also on the increase. If correct, this means that over 100 million *more* children in the 5–14 age group are now not in school than in 1970 – even while the percentage enrolled has gone up from 44 to 48%.

A further implication of these figures is that at any given time over half the Third World's children are still not at school. This may be too pessimistic: other sources suggest that a clear majority do now get at least some schooling (over 60% in 1975, according to World Bank data.) Whatever the figure, it seems that the much touted goal of universal primary education is still a long way off. Also clear is the high *unevenness* of educational provision within the Third World, in terms of just about any dimension of stratification you care to name: regional, class, ethnic, gender, or urban-rural. This will be further examined in a separate section.

Not only is primary education coverage incomplete, but thereafter Third World schooling is sharply pyramid-shaped. Only a very small proportion go on from each stage to the next, so once again there is a striking gap between percentage and absolute numbers. Undoubtedly there has been advance. *Secondary* school enrolments rose by no less than 920% between 1950–1975, which means they grew twice as fast as primary enrolments. (In many cases, this reflected a rapid post-independence expansion of secondary education, in countries like Zambia, to fill the huge gaps left by the colonial education system.)

Yet even the most developed Third World countries rarely have even half of the relevant age group in secondary school. Usually the figure is much lower than this. It is ironic, then, that *budgets* catering for this minority are often higher than those for the entire primary school system (which is all the education the majority will ever get). Secondary schools are typically much better equipped and staffed.

Similar considerations apply even more forcefully to tertiary or *higher* education. Universities are often the most expensive sector of the lot (in part inevitably so, since they need laboratories, etc.), even though they serve only a tiny minority. Here too there have been dramatic percentage increases, as newly independent countries set up new universities in order to turn out indigenous replacements for colonial expatriates. Yet, to put things in proportion, even despite a tenfold increase in numbers of Third World students between 1950 and 1975, the South still lags far behind the North. In all LDCs, in 1970, there were less than 6 million students; while the developed countries, despite their smaller overall population, had over 20 million.

Besides the school and college system, what other developments have there been? Perhaps understandably, provision of special schools or pre-school education is deemed a luxury in most of the Third World, except for some communist countries. (North Korea claims to be the first country in the world with 100% creche and kindergarten provision.) So the only major area of non-school educational activity has been *adult education*, especially in relation to *literacy*. Global literacy rates do indicate progress: illiteracy went down from 44% in 1950 to 34% in 1970, and the trend continues. On the other hand, most of this is probably due more to expanding primary education than working with existing adults. There are estimated to be still some 800 million people (of whom at least 60% are women) who cannot read and write. And, as we saw with other statistics, here too the absolute numbers may be growing even while the percentage declines. Only in socialist countries like Cuba or Tanzania have mass literacy campaigns, aimed at adults, noticeably dented the existing illiteracy statistics.

Education and Inequality

The inadequacies of educational provision in the Third World become even starker if we break down national or global data into particular real groups, and consider their *access* (or lack of it) to education.

By *region*, first of all, educational coverage is much better (especially at primary level) in most of Asia and Latin America than in much of Africa. The most developed Third World countries, especially in East Asia, have enrolment figures little worse than those in the West – i.e. almost universal education.

Within particular countries, however, there arise several different dimensions of unequal access. A major one is *urban/rural*. Almost without exception, there is more and better educational provision in city than in countryside – even though most of the population are rural. Sometimes the differences are stark: Buchanan (1975, p. 29) claims that in the West African state of Mali only 3% of rural children got any education at all – compared with 75% in the capital, Bamako.

Gender is also an important aspect of inequality in this as in most other spheres of existence. Almost all enrolment rates everywhere, except in the richest LDCs, show a lower proportion of girls than of boys in school. Although there has been progress, the drop-out rate for girls still tends to be higher; and the sex gap increases at secondary and higher levels.

A particularly difficult and often divisive problem is that of *ethnicity*. Most Third World nation-states incorporate within their boundaries a number (in some cases, a large number) of different ethnic groups. This raises a number of educational problems. The most difficult of these concerns *language*, and a separate section is devoted to this. But even apart from language, different peoples may for historical reasons have (or believe they have) unequal access to education: minorities (especially remote ones) claim they are excluded by the majority, and so on. (Of course, such problems are not confined to the Third World. In Western Europe, too, old national minorities and new immigrant communities alike often feel they get a raw deal from the education system.)

Last but by no means least, there is *class*. Controversy rages as to how or how far you can apply class analysis (Marxist or otherwise) in the often very different context of non-Western societies. Suffice it to say that, in the Third World just like everywhere else, those individuals or groups who have wealth and status and power (on whatever basis) seem well placed to ensure that their children get in and get on better than other people's in the education system. In other words, *social mobility* is as constrained in the Third World as anywhere else – probably more so, in many cases, since inequalities of all sorts are often harsher in the South than in the North (another reason, incidentally, why 'averages' of e.g. GNP per head can be very misleading).

Any exceptions are likely to be few and temporary: for example, Szentes' (in Cliffe and Saul, 1973, p. 341ff) interesting argument that, in Tanzania and similar then newly independent countries, a rapidly expanding bureaucracy and education system entailed large-scale elite recruitment from the sons and daughters of peasants, simply because there wasn't anybody else; and that this prevented crystallization of a closed ruling class. However, any such expansion has now ceased, and it would take a brave optimist to maintain that recruitment of subsequent generations of the elite would remain so broad-based.

Two last brief comments on all these inequalities: they reinforce one another and they get worse the higher you go in the education system. The boy child of a wealthy urban elite family, belonging to a dominant ethnic group, has educational opportunities almost infinitely better than a girl from a poor rural minority tribe. And even if that girl makes it to and through primary school, what chance has she got at secondary level? – which may well mean leaving home and moving to the city, to be taught in a language not her own; even while rich boy stays on his home ground, and learns in the language he speaks at home anyway. Small wonder if poor girl's parents put pressure on her to stay home, help in the house and on the farm, and then get married ... In such ways do Third World education systems, like those elsewhere, serve – wittingly or not – to reproduce and reinforce existing social inequalities.

A Relevant Education?

So far we've mostly considered educational provision in *quantitative* terms: numbers enrolled, and so forth. However, the *qualitative* dimension is also very important, i.e. how good is the education? Some aspects of this are fairly straightforward. Most Third World educational facilities are much less well equipped than in the West, and their teachers may well be less qualified too. As ever, the problems are most acute at primary schools; many of which suffer from excessive pupil-teacher ratios, severe shortages of equipment, ageing or inadequate facilities, and poorly trained teachers.

Over and above such matters, however, there remains the crucial question: what *kind* of education do people get in the Third World? and is it the kind they *should* be getting? These are difficult and controversial issues. Partly, it is a debate about priorities. We have already noted that often more money gets spent on the few enjoying secondary and higher education, than on the many who will know only primary school. But some critics go further, arguing that the *content* of education is also inappropriate – too 'academic', geared to the few who will go on to secondary school, and hence having nothing to say to the great majority whose lot will be to return to the slum or the farm.

It gets worse. Not only does schooling not help the majority but it actually does them a disservice – by encouraging aspirations to urban lifestyles and white-collar careers which the system can't in fact deliver. Education is thus blamed, not only for not being relevant to agriculture, but for putting people off farming in any case and filling their heads with all kinds of fancy ideas.

Even the education received by the privileged few who do leap the hurdle into secondary school and beyond can be criticized. Still too much book-learning, not enough practicality; too much arts, too little science and engineering; too much oriented around the old colonial power, too little devoted to one's own country. There is surely much truth in this, even though it is hard to generalize and things do change. Many West Indians did indeed suffer geography lessons that taught them more about Britain than the Caribbean. And even in Tanzania, the one and only university started life in the early 1960s with a Faculty of Law, of all things; and didn't acquire a Faculty of Engineering until a decade later.

Going back to the debate about primary education, however, there is a real dilemma. Even if the critics are right, what is to be done? Already in colonial times in East Africa there were some attempts to suggest a more agriculturally-based primary school curriculum – but these were roundly condemned by the rising nationalist movements as an insidious plot to confine Africans forever to the role of hewers of wood and drawers of water. Yet now the nationalists are in power, they too face the same problem. Any move towards a more practical primary education, such as President Nyerere of Tanzania has advocated, runs the risk of still being interpreted as an attempt to 'freeze' and preserve existing inequalities of access and life-chances.

Yet if nothing is done and things go on as they are, the more visible become the perverse effects described by Ronald Dore (1976) as *The Diploma Disease*. (Other terms for the same sort of things include 'qualificationism', 'certification', and 'credentialism'.) Where the demand for jobs greatly exceeds the supply, educational qualifications – say, a primary school leaving certificate – seem like a simpler way of selecting candidates than actually trying to test whether they have relevant abilities or skills. Those who lose out in this process are likely to respond by staying in the education system, re-sitting until they pass; while others stay on to move up a stage and acquire O-levels, and so be better placed. This of course ups the ante for everybody; now, you need O-levels to get a job. And so on . . .

In the end, even a country like Sri Lanka (poor, but with an extensive education system) winds up producing excess numbers of unemployed university graduates! – who still can't get jobs, because there are scarcely more jobs around than there were in the first place; and whose paper 'credentials' (which haven't delivered the goods for them in any case) bear no necessary relation to the possession of any useable or useful skills. It's an ironic and gloomy picture. Despite surface similarities, Dore is careful to distance his critique from 'trendy de-schoolers' like Ivan Illich. Far from wanting to abolish schools, his concern is that they should do their job better – if they can only get away from the 'formalism' and 'ritualism' which the wild goose chase after exam success and the attendant piece of paper imposes upon them.

Education, Economics and Development

The foregoing discussion has highlighted the relationship (or lack of it) between education and the economy, in terms of employment structures and prospects (or, again, the lack of them). This can be looked at from either a micro- or a macro-perspective: as individuals see it, or as governments.

As to the former, individuals are not wrong in this perception of differential rewards for the educated few. Silvey (in MacPherson, 1982, p. 78) cites a study which estimated a graduate's earnings to be more than six times those of a primary school leaver. But so narrow is the apex of the pyramid that the vast majority are doomed never to make it, and hence to disappointment.

Governments have often experienced a not dissimilar frustration, as their macro-calculations go awry. In retrospect, during the 1960s, too much faith was placed in education as *automatically* producing the 'human capital' that would promote development; just as earlier, in the 1950s, it was thought that *real* capital alone – 'aid' – would do the trick. Today, it is recognized that creating formal employment is a problem in its own right.

Yet it seems reasonable that there should be *some* connection between education, employment and development. The problem is that it is not easy to establish the precise linkages. Bairoch (1975) noted that the now developed countries had their own industrial revolutions in the nineteenth century with mostly very low literacy rates (technologies were simpler then, admittedly). The same author cites studies from the early USSR as suggesting, nonetheless, that increased literacy does more for industrial productivity than formal apprenticeships. (This may add an economic reason to the political and social motives for socialist regimes, e.g. in Cuba, Nicaragua and Somalia, to conduct massive literacy campaigns as one of the first steps in their development strategy.)

Inevitably, however, there is a timelag before the benefits of better education show up in the economy. And still the exact relations can be hard to specify. Anderson and Bowman (cited in Hardiman and Midgley, 1982, p. 201) find certain correlations. 40% literacy seems to be a kind of threshold, in that the very poorest countries are mostly below this. At the other end of the scale, the richest Third World countries tend to have literacy rates of 80% and above. But in between there is no very clear correlation. As they suggest, GNP alone is too crude a figure; one must also look at income distribution, demographic factors, and above all the structure of employment.

Over most of the Third World demand for education remains high, despite the fact that in many cases (especially for secondary and higher education) people have to pay for it – as is also the case with health services. Yet educated unemployment (e.g. jobless school leavers) is also well-nigh universal in the South, sometimes alongside a lack of skilled human power in particular sectors. In conclusion, education may well be a necessary but is certainly not a sufficient condition for development, both economically and socially. In particular, expanding education and hoping for the best is no substitute for direct measures to create jobs.

Language and Education

When I taught at the University of Dar es Salaam in the early 1970s, I had the convenience of teaching in my own language: English is the official medium of instruction in higher and secondary education in Tanzania. For the students, however, English (which they wrote at least as well as British students) was not even their second but their *third* language. They will have grown up speaking one of Tanzania's several dozen vernaculars (local languages), such as Chagga or Ha, and then learned in Swahili, the national African language, at primary school before switching to English at secondary level.

Similar situations are by no means rare in the Third World. Although Swahili has few equivalents, the choice between vernacular and national languages as a medium of educational instruction has many aspects and is not easy. Suppose you have vernacular primary education; after all, children learn best in the language they're used to. What about secondary school? Quite possibly, by that stage children from different language groups may be studying alongside each other (they certainly will at university). Obviously they can't all be taught in different languages. What then?

Almost certainly, some language groups (peoples, 'tribes') will be bigger than others. Should minorities then learn the majority's language? and learn everything else *in* it? Where there is one dominant group and relatively few or small minorities, that is indeed what tends to happen. (And not only in the Third World: earlier in this century, you could be beaten in Wales or Scotland if heard to speak Welsh or Gaelic in schools.) But if there are a number of groups, this would be both impracticable and politically controversial: each group will be fearful of others gaining too much power, so to elevate any one such language to be *the* language of education would be to stir up a hornet's nest.

And that is why over large parts of the ex-colonial world, especially Africa, the official language (of education, and otherwise) remains that of the former colonial power: English, French or Portuguese. That way, no one indigenous language gets privileged: all are equal. It has other advantages too. Much of the world's scientific and academic literature is written in English or French, so to choose one of these as an educational medium saves an awful lot of translating. (In Tanzania lip-service is paid to the goal of ultimately 'Swahilianizing' the whole education system, and the Institute of Kiswahili Research is busy inventing technical terms – 'sociology' is 'elimu ya ujami'. But somehow one wonders whether, or when, it will actually happen.)

Adopting a European language has its negative side, however. For one thing, it disadvantages those unfamiliar with it – which is another way of saying that it gives yet another boost to those from privileged homes, where English or French may already be familiar. Similarly, for those alarmed about cultural dependency, it drives yet another wedge between the elites and their fellow-citizens, while simultaneously cementing further their ties with the former colonial power.

In some former colonies, 'pidgins' or 'creoles' have developed as a spontaneous mix of elements of European and indigenous languages. Yet even in such cases, such as Guinea-Bissau (the former Portuguese Guinea), governments have usually preferred to adopt the 'pure' European language for official and educational use. A partial exception is Papua New Guinea, that extraordinary country with its hundreds of language groups, where 'Tok Pisin' (talk pidgin) has official status alongside English.

It is tempting to multiply illustrations. Complicated political games can be played out in the realm of language. In Malaysia, for instance, Malays worried about Chinese predominance in the education system brought in proficiency in the Malay language as a qualification for university entrance – which is one reason why many Malaysian Chinese come to study in the UK. In Hong Kong, a longstanding debate as to which of English or Chinese should be the medium of instruction (there are universities which use each) will doubtless receive fresh momentum as the territory's reversion to China in 1997 draws nearer. And so on . . . There are endless examples, but no easy answers.

Polemics and Practitioners: Illich and Freire

It would be wrong to close this chapter without at least mentioning two major and much discussed figures who have helped shape thinking about educational problems in the Third World. Of the two, Ivan Illich is the better known. An Austrian who lives in Mexico, his radical diagnosis of and prescriptions for schools (and indeed many other conventional institutions) are famous beyond the Third World. Arguing that most people learn most of what they know (and what it is actually useful to know) outside school rather than within it, Illich goes so far as to recommend – in the title of his most famous book – 'deschooling society'. Learning and teaching should be a co-operative endeavour, and a lifetime process, occupying (say) two months a year over a 20–30 year period rather than all being squashed up front during the few years of childhood.

By contrast, the ideas of the Brazilian Paulo Freire embody a perhaps more workable radicalism. They were certainly developed in practice: Freire was formerly in charge of his country's National Literacy Programme, and insisted that literacy could only be effectively promoted among the poorest if it was linked explicitly to thinking critically about their own situation and what they might do about it. In a word (and a word unpronouncable in any language), this entails a process of *consciencization*: not just consciousness–raising, but people learning to think and act as subjects in their own right.

Needless to say, none of this went down a bomb with the right wing military dictatorship which seized power in Brazil in 1964; they closed down Freire's programme, and exiled him.

Cultural Dependency?

Let us now return to the idea of 'education as cultural imperalism' – itself the title of a book by Martin Carnoy. The basic point is tellingly put by a Senegalese writer, Sheikh Hamidou Kane (quoted in Buchanan, 1975, p. 31): 'More effectively than the gun, it makes conquest permanent. The gun coerces the body, but the school bewitches the mind'.

There is undoubtedly much in the Third World's historical experience which chimes in with this view. In colonial times, Western (often missionary) education could be profoundly culturally divisive, splitting communities and even families. In a classic study, Mayer (1963) reported how in a South African city urban Xhosa saw themselves as belonging to one or two opposed groups. *Red* were those who still wore the traditional ochre of their nation, and in general kept up their old beliefs and customs. The others, more westernized in their lifestyles, religion, and so forth were significantly called *School*. Similar episodes, differing in degree and detail, could be quoted from the length and breadth of the Third World.

And indeed beyond: for wherever 'modernity' came from the outside (whether or not at the barrel of a gun), it has always involved profound cultural conflict and agonising choices. Thus Rusisian intellectuals over a century ago found themselves divided into 'Westernizers' and 'Panslavists': the former arguing that only wholesale and immediate adoption of Western science, education and institutions could save Russia, the latter insisting that on the contrary it was essential to reaffirm whatever traditions made Russia unique and different. In the coming decades, Arab, Chinese and many other intelligentsias would each independently repeat the terms of this debate.

In retrospect, then, it showed astonishing optimism or ignorance or both for modernization theorists to assume that such cultural change was relatively unproblematical. Although it was admitted there would be 'strains', Lerner's claims in the mid 1950s that 'what America is, the modernizing Middle East now seeks to become', and his view of Islam as defenceless against the 'rationalist and positivist spirit' look bizarre in the mid 1980s, with a virulently anti-American Islamic neo-fundamentalism riding high in Iran and elsewhere.

Even so, I'm not convinced that the 'cultural dependence' school have got it quite right either. That there has been a continuing process of cultural Westernization of the Third World seems to me an undeniable fact. To some extent, how we evaluate it ethically seems to me beside the point, since at least some aspects are irreversible. For example, despite Illich schools are not actually going to be abolished in the Third World. So whether or not it was a good thing for Western-style education to come to dominate the Third World is really beside the point; it's there, and that's that. The point is that much that *was* foreign in the Third World has now taken root, to the extent that it is no longer useful or proper to regard it as other than indigenous. Religion is the obvious case: both Christianity and Islam are in a sense 'foreign' to everywhere outside Palestine and Saudi Arabia respectively, yet it would be sociologically ludicrous today to think in such terms. Similarly, no one is actually going to unpick the patterns that imperialism has woven upon our world. Dye them a different colour, perhaps. But things are not going to go back.

Yet people do muse upon these things, like the Russians I mentioned. And in this, I think, lies the Third World's salvation. It can, and in some sense always does, *react*: select, redefine, recombine cultural elements from many sources – its own traditions (themselves no single seamless web) and various newer influences (equally diverse). There is of course nothing automatic or evolutionary about this. It involves debate and cultural contestation – like Chileans under the Allende government rediscovering and reasserting their Indian musical inheritance, against the tide of Tin Pan Alley. That sort of thing is happening all the time, producing new syntheses (like the music of Inti Illimani) which surely enhance the whole world's cultural heritage.

In sum, if modernization theory couldn't see the problem, dependency couldn't see the solution. Modernization is never pure and naked: it always wears particular cultural clothes. But these garments are not necessarily straitjackets. Some put them on others; but the wearers usually adopt and transform them, and may well make them fit.

Chapter Nine

Women and Development

Introduction

Until quite recently gender issues were conspicuous by their absence from the sociology of development as with most of the rest of sociology. And, as in other areas, the gradual process of making amends for this astonishing oversight is proving very fruitful for the sociology of development, in two ways. Not only is it a matter of filling a gap, painting in a blank, putting in something which was left out. But perhaps even more importantly, awareness of a gender dimension often sheds new light on other already 'known' areas of sociology too. Where appropriate, in the various substantive chapters in this book I try to draw attention to gender-related aspects. But there is need also for a chapter in its own right on women, although inevitably this will only scratch the surface of what is if anything an even wider range of issues than usual.

Let us begin with some facts and figures. Women form 50% of the world's population; perhaps fractionally more, since on average they live longer than men. It is estimated that this half of us work two-thirds of all work hours in the world, and are responsible for 50% of world food production. Yet they receive only 10% of world income, and own a derisory 1% of world property. They have other obligations, too: one-third of all families are headed by women.

In Africa in particular, for example, women do 60–80% of all agricultural work, 50% of animal husbandry, and close on 100% of food processing. Or again, to break down an often quoted 'global' figure, of the world's 800 million illiterates, 3 out of 5 (480 million) are women. Illiteracy is in fact increasing, and once again the process is unequal by gender. During the 1970s male illiteracy grew by about 2 million p.a.; for females, the figure was 5 million p.a.

I mentioned in Chapter 7 (p. 81) that women tend to live longer than men. In the First World where at least physical conditions (if not social conditions) for the sexes are relatively equal, the lifespan gap can be up to eight years. In the Third World, reflecting the enormous physical burdens which fall disproportionately upon women, this gap falls to two years. In India and Bangladesh it is actually reversed, and men survive longer than women.

Women in Development

Like other themes in this book, women's subordination has both economic, political, and cultural aspects. Also, given that Third World societies today are a mix of traditional and modern, internal and external influences, it is important to stress that *all* these can be sources of inequality. It would be equally wrong, in my view, to portray Third World women as uniformly sunk in bondage until rescued by the progressive West, as it would be to reverse the picture and conceive of the South as a utopia of sexual egalitarianism until evil capitalism came and brought in oppression. The real picture is much more complicated.

Some of the complexities and ambiguities are summarized by Paul Harrison (1981, p. 438ff). In general, women work a 'double day': not only eight hours or more in formal labour outside the home, but often the same amount of domestic labour within it. Lest any man still associates women's work with 'light' work, Harrison points out that three well-nigh universal and back-breaking tasks – fetching water, gathering fire wood, and grinding corn – are almost invariably performed by women. That much may be traditional, but the same is not true of other factors working to render women 'the poorest of the poor' (the title of Harrison's chapter).

Thus it is modern factory-produced consumer goods (whether made in the Third World, or imported from the West) which have dealt a body blow to indigenous handicraft production – often a traditional livelihood for women. Or again, it is modern systems of male labour migration which have redoubled the burdens upon women, who are left holding the fort in every sense – running the farm single-handed, bringing up children, etc. – while their menfolk migrate to cities or even overseas for long periods in search of wage employment. And it is well meant but ill conceived modern rural development projects which, as Barbara Rogers (1980) has illustrated, time and again benefit men whilst excluding or even harming women. Mechanization of ploughing, for instance, lightens men's load as this is usually a male task – while simultaneously putting far more pressure on other jobs, e.g. weeding and processing, which are done by women but which do not receive the benefit of mechanization.

Women and Life-chances

What sorts of factors should we look at, in order to assess and indeed compare the positions of women in different societies? Blumberg (quoted in Giele, 1977) lists seven 'life options': whether and whom to marry; termination of such unions; sexual freedom, before and outside marriage; freedom of movement; access to educational opportunities; power within the household; and control over reproduction and family size. On each of these, one can compare the position of men and women both within and across societies. Thus, on sexual freedom hypocrisy and double standards are well-nigh universal. A man (married or not) who 'sleeps around' rarely incurs any penalty, and may even earn unofficial kudos ('he's a bit of a lad'); whereas a woman who does exactly the same risks at best insults ('slag', and worse), or at worst in some societies severe punishment or even death.

Blumberg's seven criteria, however, mostly focus on household and family. Yet this is only part of the picture, and Giele provides a more comprehensive sixfold list of different spheres. First is *political expression*. What rights do women possess, formally and otherwise? Can they vote, in theory and practice? Can they own property in their own right? Can they express any dissatisfactions in their own movements? Second is *work and mobility*. How do women fare in the formal labour force? How mobile are they; how well are they paid, how are their jobs ranked, and what leisure do they get?

Third comes *family: formation, duration, and size*. Do women choose their own partners? Can they divorce them? What is the status of single women and widows? Do women have freedom of movement? Fourth is *education*; what access do women have, how much can they attain, and is the curriculum the same? Fifth is *health and sexual control*: what is women's mortality, to what particular illnesses and stresses (physical and mental) are they exposed, and what control do they have over their own fertility? Last, elusive but important, there is what Giele calls *cultural expression*. What images of women and their 'place' are prevalent, and how far do these reflect or determine the reality? And what can women do in the cultural field? In the next section, we shall briefly examine some of these issues in particular regions of the Third World.

Variations by Region

Although as Rosaldo and Lamphere have said 'sexual asymmetry is presently a universal fact of human social life' (quoted in Giele, 1977), nonetheless, both the forms and degrees of women's subordination vary greatly, from place to place and over time. In both respects the Third World is no exception, as the following (inevitably highly selective and compressed) thumb-nail sketch may indicate.

In many parts of *Africa*, women traditionally had more power and status than was the case in much of South and East Asia, or even in Europe. They had major socio-economic roles, as farmers, producers of craft goods, and traders – this last remaining important today, as with the market women in several West African societies. Also, women often participated in political decision-making through their own organizations. Some societies had female chiefs.

By contrast, in many *Islamic societies* (in West and South Asia, and North Africa) the role segregation and subordination of women was and is considerable. In extreme cases, the practice of *purdah* delineates largely separate spheres for men and women, corresponding to the 'public' and 'private' realms respectively. Women's participation in public life ranges from limited to non-existent. Often, even to enter the public domain (e.g. walk in the street) requires varying degrees of veiling. Although there is much variation, it may be salutary for anyone who thinks of development as automatically unilinear and progressive to note that, with the current wave of fundamentalist revival within Islam, even in hitherto more relaxed societies like Malaysia women are coming under increasing pressure to don the veil.

In *East Asian* societies the cultural heritage of Confucianism emphasized the subordination of women as one of the several parallel 'natural' hierarchies: young to old, children to parents, ruled to rulers. Although to a degree transformed by socialist revolution in some countries and capitalist industrialization in others, such norms are persistent. In South Korea, for instance, although women's education is far better provided for than in most of the Third World, it is hard for graduate women to find jobs, let alone make careers, and the pressure to marry is acute. And the divorce position is Victorian: although legal, it is rare because considered shameful – and the *father*, as head of household, is almost certain to win custody of children if he wishes. Working-class women face different problems. Far from being excluded from the formal labour force, millions work as factory workers – yet their pay averages less than half what men get, which is itself not high. And, on top of long hours of factory work, women as everywhere have primary responsibility for child care and running the home as well.

Women's position in *Latin America* is ambivalent. Saffiotti (in Rohrlich-Leavitt, 1975) suggests that the ideology of 'machismo' has effects in the sphere of women and work. Women are regarded as and socialized into being wives and mothers, dedicated to self-sacrifice. Wage labour is viewed as secondary, and not relieving them from these primary domestic obligations. Both from the viewpoint of society and their own husbands, therefore, women are seen as available to be pushed either into or out of the formal labour market as and when necessary. Such jobs as they do get, like elsewhere in the world, tend to be the worst paid and defined as the least skilled: in factories, as vendors, or domestic service. The last involves a particular irony. One plus for Latin America is that it has a rather larger proportion of middle-class women pursuing professional careers than is normal elsewhere in the Third World. Yet this is only possible because of the availability of other women to perform low-paid domestic service and child care.

Women in Historical Development

The recent growth of interest in gender issues in sociology has led to much research and speculation on the position of women in long-run processes of historical change. Some radical feminists have pictured an original human condition of matriarchy, but evidence for this is scarce.

What does seem plausible, however, is a relationship between different types of society (especially in agriculture) and the position of women changing – not always for the better. Ester Boserup (1970) put forward a theory relating to different ecological contexts. Hunting and gathering societies, first, have a relatively low sexual division of labour. Once settled agriculture begins, the pattern varies. Hoe-based agriculture and shifting cultivation, especially in Africa, seem to be related to an increase not only in women's role in farming but also in their political autonomy. Conversely, the introduction of dry plough agriculture is almost always associated with men's labour, as this is 'heavy' work; and women come to experience restrictions also on their mobility and commercial activities. However, the pattern is different in wet, paddy farming (notably rice). There, tasks necessary for intensive cultivation (irrigation, weeding, transplanting, etc.) ensure an important role for women in production, and concomitant status.

Although generalizing of this kind is always hazardous, it is a merit of Boserup's approach that it is not so much a 'stage' theory as one related to different environmental contexts. We could say: progress is neither unilinear (one way) nor is it indeed necessarily progressive (for the better). By contrast, it seems in many ways too simple to reduce this as Giele (1977) does to a three-stage general model of women's social position: from early high status (often very long ago indeed), via a lengthy period of constriction – most of recorded human history, in fact – to a prospect of some improvements in the present era.

It should be said, however, that this alleged 'curvilinear relationship between societal complexity and sex equality' (up, down, then up again) appears to be paralleled in the obviously related area of changing family structures. The standard view which associated the nuclear family with modern industrialism and the extended family with pre-industrial societies has been subject to a number of criticisms and qualifications. The one which concerns us here suggests that the very earliest hunter and gatherer societies also had something like a simple nuclear family structure; and that only with plough-based agriculture did the extended family, under a male patriarchal 'head of household', arise.

Women, Colonialism and Economic Change

The effects of colonialism on the position of women were not clear-cut. There were those who saw themselves as striving to rescue women from traditional forms of oppression. Missionaries in Kenya, for instance, caused controversy by forbidding the practice of female circumcision among their converts. In Korea, education for women was virtually founded by Christian missionaries. On the other hand, almost by definition missionaries brought with them their own Western ideas about 'women's place', thus introducing new forms of inequality (e.g. seeing women's roles as primarily domestic).

Other aspects of the impact on women of broader economic changes have already been mentioned, such as pressure on handicraft production and the rise of migrant labour. The latter should not be underestimated, especially in Africa, and its effects continue to loom large today. Millions of women do not see their husbands, or only very briefly, for months or years at a stretch. By no means all of them receive much in the way of cash remittances from male earnings. Meanwhile, they must look after farms and bring up their children alone – or with only the help of the elderly. In South Africa, notoriously, such arrangements are legally formalized in 'pass laws' and so-called 'homelands'. Elsewhere – including neighbouring independent countries which still supply labour to South Africa – economic pressures produce a not dissimilar result.

Even so, modernization theorists would doubtless stress the way in which development has transformed women's position and options out of all recognition. The rise of urban life, the increase in educational access, the opportunities for factory and other formal labour, all constitute major changes. Yet a rounded view must surely emphasize the unevenness and contradictions attendant upon such processes. To gain such advantages, women must not only often fight against concepts of their traditional role, but usually even if 'successful' they must continue to perform the lion's share of domestic labour as well. Factory work is a particularly ambiguous area, in which the price of gaining some measure of autonomy and income of one's own is often submission to new forms of exploitation: long hours, low wages, and the advances of chauvinist male bosses.

In India, poor peasant women work in the fields alongside men. One of the first social consequences of agrarian prosperity, for instance in the Punjab under the influence of the Green Revolution, is for wealthier farmers to show their new status by withdrawing 'their' women from agricultural labour – and keeping them in the home. Is this progress, for the women concerned?

Women in Export Manufacturing

As already implied, gender issues in the Third World are not just one 'area' among others. Rather, they raise questions that run the gamut of the entire development process: old and new, traditional and modern, internal and external, economic, political and cultural.

A striking modern example concerns the increasing numbers of young women, notably in South and East Asia and Latin America, who now work in factories producing goods (mainly textiles and electronics) for export to world markets. This is a trend of the 1970s and 1980s involving both 'footloose' Western TNCS and indigenous Third World firms. What is noteworthy in many cases is their positive preference for labour which is young (aged 14–25), female, and often newly recruited to the formal labour-force. How can we explain this new trend, and how is it liable to affect women's positions?

Diane Elson and Ruth Pearson (in Young et al, 1981) have made a particular study of these issues. At one level, capital seeks labour that is cheaper, pliable, and docile. Third World labour in general may well fulfil these criteria; especially in countries which offer to TNCs the 'carrot' of EPZs (export processing zones) with all their incentives, plus the 'stick' to the workforce of suppressing trades unionism. Young female labour may be especially suitable. But, importantly, the categories and labels used should not be taken at face value; they require historical explanation. Thus, if women are 'docile' (and they aren't always: world market factories in several countries have seen some explosive strikes, sit-ins, lock-outs, etc.), this may be partly a mask they put on in order to survive – like black slaves who pretended to be cheerful 'Uncle Toms'. Or it may represent a deference to authority already inculcated by traditional patriarchal structures, which capital can then adapt to its own uses and circumstances – e.g. by employing male bosses and supervisors, as is normally the case. Similarly, it is because of what Elson and Pearson refer to as women's 'material subordination as a gender' that women may also put up with lower wages, or accept a high rate of labour turnover – because they know they are going to leave and get married in any case.

The question of *skill* is of especial sociological interest. In this field as elsewhere, work that women do is typically classified as 'unskilled', and paid accordingly. Insofar as any element of skill *is* admitted, it is attributed to women's nature. Thus Elson and Pearson quote an official Malaysian brochure soliciting foreign investment, which manages to be both racist and sexist in claiming that 'the manual dexterity of the Oriental female is famous the world over'. The truth is that many women do indeed have these skills, not by nature but learned from other women in the household – and hence not recognized as skills to the patriarchal powers that be.

What are the consequences? Elson and Pearson suggest that there are three possible outcomes, and that factory work may either *intensify, decompose,* or *recompose* pre-existing forms of gender subordination. It is an empirical question, and examples of all three (as well as mixed forms) have been found. Intensification of subordination could be where wages are not even paid to the women themselves, but to their fathers. Alternatively, in the second case, decomposition of subordination, some women may use the money they make from factory work to increase their own autonomy, e.g. by getting out of the need for an arranged marriage. Or, in the third case, recomposition of subordination, it's old wine in new bottles. Nothing really changes; male dominance appears in a new form (e.g. women workers, male bosses).

But change it is, nevertheless. Elson and Pearson stress the negative aspects. Long bouts of shiftwork take their toll; stitching copper wires onto silicon chips can induce severe eyestrain. Moreover, dependence on the world market may be unstable anyway. Women who have reshaped their lives around wage income and then lose their job may face a bleak future, with little choice but to seek to survive in the service sector – which may in practice entail prostitution or related activities.

After the Revolution? Women in Socialist Countries

One obvious question is to ask how far and with what success the many and varied problems outlined above have been tackled in countries which claim adherence to socialism. Maxine Molyneux (in Young *et al* eds, 1981) has surveyed the position in a number of the countries we conventionally call 'communist'. She found a mixed picture, in which at least four things were generally positive.

In the first place, and not to be discounted, there is official ideological commitment to equality of the sexes. What this means in practice is admittedly varied. Among Islamic societies, whereas supposedly socialist regimes like those in Algeria, Libya or Somalia offered little more than lip-service, it was the avowedly Marxist-Leninist regimes like those in Afghanistan, South Yemen (formerly Aden), and Soviet Central Asia which had actually dared to tackle such traditions as polygyny (two or more wives), child marriage, the veil, and seclusion of women in general.

Secondly, entrance into the formal labour market is seen at least in principle as a normal expectation, even a duty, for women as well as men. Thirdly, there is commitment to full employment and mobilizing women; while in general, fourthly, such governments accept greater responsibility than those elsewhere in the Third World, both for the reproduction of a labour force and for social welfare.

On the other hand, state socialist regimes make little attempt to change relations *within* the home. If women are drafted into the formal labour force while still bearing the brunt of household tasks, this of course continues the 'double day'. Moreover, a particular form of family tends not only to be assumed but even idealized: gender-typing abounds, especially in images and ideologies of motherhood (or conversely, male leaders as 'fathers of the nation'). Finally, women still play less part in political life, and are heavily under-represented in the topmost echelons of power.

Interesting confirmation of some of Molyneux's analysis comes from the case of Vietnam, studied by Christine White (1982). In the period 1945–1975, during three decades of almost continuous war against first France and then the USA, the role of women in North Vietnam was crucial – to the point where by the end they were responsible for nearly all agriculture and the greater part of industrial production as well, and large numbers had acquired Party membership. After victory in 1975, however, not only did many women in leadership positions lose their jobs to newly demobilized men (which also happened in the West, after 1945), but party cards were called in and re-issued. The new issue gave preference to army veterans who are of course overwhelmingly male. (As an aside, but a very important one: the ways in which *military* regimes and the militarization of societies – common in the Third World – *generally* entrench and enhance specifically male power are only just beginning to be recognized.)

The case of Vietnam, though, is by no means wholly negative. Changes in agriculture mean that women are no longer unpaid family labour, and an effective marriage law reform has been implemented. Under socialism as under capitalism, there are particular gains and losses for women.

Women and Development Paradigms

Where does all this leave our twin rival perspectives, modernization and dependency? June Nash suggests (Nash and Safa, 1976) that both have tended to ignore gender issues. Modernization approaches not only simply overlook a good deal that women do (e.g. production within the home), but also duck the question of the ambiguous impact of much that passes for 'development' upon women. Dependency, meanwhile, fails to relate the external relations of structural dependence which it so much emphasizes to what is perhaps the most basic dependent relationship of all, the one which in a sense underpins all the rest – namely, that within the home. On reflection, the 'satellite that is no one's metropolis' at the bottom of Gunder Frank's metropolis-satellite chain should not be a landless labourer – but his wife. For that matter, Harrison (1981) has characterized women in general as 'the world's largest group of landless labourers'.

Women and Change

Most of the inequalities outlined above are well known to those who suffer them. Such knowledge is increasingly being articulated into action. Many countries in the Third World now contain women's movements of various kinds, which can differ in interesting ways from feminist movements in the West. A classic illustration is provided by Domitila Barrios de Chungara (in Johnson and Bernstein, 1982), a Bolivian Indian women's organizer and wife of a tin-miner, who describes how she went to an international women's conference in Mexico City and felt very alienated from the women on the platform –

as much for their elegant designer clothes, as for their insistence that men were the main problem and enemy.

By contrast, as Nash (in Nash and Safa, 1976) has put it, Third World women's movements are more likely to stress the need to transform the total process of uneven development of which women's subordination forms part. Class and sex exploitation are deeply interwoven; 'development' processes have profoundly affected women's roles; hence it seems both analytically problematical and politically inappropriate to isolate women's issues from their broader context. Not that this is a recipe for doing nothing. Such movements are no longer content to be left on the back burner, or told by men to wait until 'after the revolution'. But most would agree that, in their particular circumstances, the task is to fight with men against oppression rather than fight against men as such.

Struggle and change can take many forms, some less obvious and visible than others. An interesting argument which illustrates the pervasiveness of gender issues is provided by Adamson (1984). One of the great advances of the twentieth century, according to Adamson, is a very recent revolution in the education of girls. Only twenty years ago as few as 15% of girls received any education; whereas in 1984 three quarters of all six year old girls started school, a proportion barely lower than the figure for both sexes combined (80%). This constitutes more progress in the last twenty years than the previous 2000. For Adamson, its most radical effects have yet to be felt. As for the first time a generation of Third World women grows up where education is the norm and not the exception, they will demand more say in decision-making, at every level from the household to the state. As mothers, these educated women will have fewer children, whom they will be better able to look after – and educate in their turn. Thus improvements for women spread out and result in improvements for all in health, education, and population.

Possibly Adamson is too optimistic. Many (and disproportionately many) of those girls will drop out of school; and doubtless women's attempts to improve their lot will continue to meet resistance. In some countries, where Islamic fundamentalism is growing, the position of women may well deteriorate. Even so, I am tempted to share Adamson's sense that a mightly global social movement is now at last under way – perhaps, indeed, the mightiest of all.

Once, Marxists thought of the working-class as somehow encapsulating all exploitation, such that their liberation and overthrow of the existing order would constitute liberation for all. More recently, some 'Third Worldist' Marxists have suggested that at a global level it was the peasantry and not the proletariat who now fulfilled this vanguard role. Personally, I am sceptical (with some regret) of such dramatic visions – indeed, I think that to be able to transcend them in favour of a more complex if less dramatic world view is a sign of the maturing of sociology. Still, if I were ever tempted to see a single social group and their particular afflictions and struggles as the key to transforming our world, then for me it would be neither workers nor peasants as such, but rather those who were for so long astonishingly invisible to sociologists and socialists alike, the 'minority' who are in fact the majority: the subject of this chapter, gradually but irreversibly becoming the subject of history too.

Chapter Ten

Religion

The sociology of development has tended to neglect the rich field of Third World religion. This reflects its general over-emphasis on economic and political phenomena. Such a gap is unfortunate, since the material is both fascinating and important.

The above criticism cannot, however, be applied to social anthropology, whose opposite bias – towards the study of cultural aspects of social life – has here stood it in good stead. Of the works I shall mention, some are by anthropologists, some by sociologists, and some by historians. As always, it is far from certain that these disciplines are ultimately distinct.

The history of Third World religions can be seen in terms of hundreds or even thousands of separate cultural traditions (none of them static) coming into increasing contact with one another. This has not been an equal contact. The large-scale world religions of Christianity, Islam and Buddhism have over varying periods of time (centuries, in some cases) made substantial if uneven headway all over the globe; and this process continues.

Yet, although unequal, it is not a one-way process. Rarely are all traces of pre-Christian or pre-Islamic belief and practice submerged when a society or community converts. On the contrary, it is precisely in the 'syncretisms' or mixed forms which the Third World has produced that much of its interest lies.

Out of this potentially huge and fascinating field, I shall focus on three aspects which seem of especial interest to the wider concerns of the sociology of development. Two of them have been neatly summarized by John Goldthorpe: they concern religion as *cause* or *consequence* of economic development.

The first of these might be called, a bit irreverently, 'son of Protestant Ethic', referring to Max Weber's classic argument that capitalist development in the West was not originated by economic factors alone (although he maintained nothing so simple as that Protestantism *caused* capitalism).

Might Protestantism, or some other religious tradition, have the same dynamizing impact in the Third World as it arguably did in the West? There have been a number of studies of 'enterprising' groups along these lines. One particularly interesting current argument suggests a 'Confucian ethic'. Noting that the NICs (Newly Industrializing Countries) of East Asia, the so-called 'gang of four' or 'four little tigers' (South Korea, Taiwan, Hong Kong, Singapore) are all overwhelmingly ethnic Chinese or Confucian by tradition, this view suggests that there may be something in Confucianism conducive to rapid development. This 'something' might include: a respect for authority and the state; concern for education and learning; seeing oneself as part of a wider social whole; working together in harmony.

This may sound plausible, and certainly there is a correlation which needs explaining. However, there are problems. For one thing, Confucianism is not exactly a religion but more a social philosophy or ethic; still, for present purposes this may not matter. More damagingly, it was these very aspects that are now cited as virtues – deference, lack of individualism, etc. – which Weber in his original argument claimed could only maintain social conservatism! – inasmuch as they made innovation or rebellion impossible.

Perhaps the moral is to always be wary of single-factor explanations. Even if a Confucian ethic does act as a kind of social cement once growth is under way (and there's no doubt that the political cultures of all the East Asian NICs differ utterly from those of Brazil or Mexico, for instance), I suspect we must also look elsewhere for material, political, and other highly specific factors in explaining the total process of growth and development. Besides, Confucianism has been around for centuries, millennia even; whereas these growth processes are barely twenty years old. To explain the latter solely in terms of the former would therefore be a gross error of method. Even so, it would probably be wrong to rule such cultural factors out of the picture altogether. The challenge is how to 'operationalize' them, as part of a total explanation which can also account for why they come into play at some times but not at others.

Whether or not religion can be a cause of economic development, it has often been the subject of strikingly dramatic effects. This brings us to Goldthorpe's second category. It is by no means one confined to the Third World. On the contrary, whenever people have been faced by massive and seemingly inexplicable sudden changes in their lives, they naturally struggle to try to make sense of what is happening to them. And not infrequently, in pre-modern Europe as much as the Third World, the 'explanations' they come up with have a strongly religious cast.

For this purpose, the change could be a flood, plague, or natural disaster. Or it could be the startling and terrifying arrival of people of a colour never seen before, with seemingly magical powers over objects equally inexplicable and potent (aeroplanes, guns), who proceed to take you over and order you around. In a word, *colonialism* has been a powerful cause of specifically religious response, as have the slower but no less corrosive processes which it sets in train: changes in authority structures, in patterns of land holding, in communications, etc.

We are here in the territory of what is often called *messianic* or *millenarian* religion. The technical difference is that the former looks to a particular individual saviour, now or in the future, to deliver his or her people from their travails; while the latter anticipates a second coming or new kingdom. As this vocabulary would imply, millenarianism (I shall now use this as the general term) is very much a product of the impact of Christianity, usually in the context of European colonialism.

Sometimes colonialism alone provides the spur. Perhaps the most striking example is the 'cargo cults' or Melanesia in the Pacific, described by Peter Worsley in his book *The Trumpet Shall Sound*. In brief, noticing how the European colonialists were endlessly supplied with all their needs by air, members of these cults went through the motions of clearing their own airstrips and performing what they regarded as appropriate rituals, in order that they too might receive supplies of 'cargo'.

The forms of millenarianism can be extremely diverse. One highly visible expression is the growth, in colonies or ex-colonies, after a number of years of proselytizing by missionaries, of 'breakaway' indigenous churches and sects. (In South Africa alone, significantly, there are several hundred of these.) Sometimes these regard themselves as the true church, from which the 'white man's church' has strayed. Or again, they may be more or less *syncretist*: i.e. merging elements of Christianity with aspects of indigenous religion or culture which the missionaries' Christianity would want them to reject.

Often these syncretisms are associated with active social movements, leading in some cases to open political rebellion: e.g. the Taiping in 19th century China, the Tonghak in Korea at the turn of the century, or Kimbanguism and many other cases in Africa this century. Rebellion, naturally, invites the full force of government suppression (colonial or otherwise). Because of this aspect, some commentators have stressed the political aspect and significance of millenarianism, as often an early stage in what will later become secular nationalism. Vittorio Lanternari has thus dubbed them as 'religions of the oppressed'. Other explanations are closer to modernization theory. J. Milton Yinger sees millenarian cults as a kind of 'bridge' between traditional world views and the impact of the modern world, hence helping people to cope and assisting the passage from one to another.

The final aspect on which I want to focus is related to this second one. In a nutshell: how do we explain the Ayatollah? For a very striking feature of parts of the contemporary Third World is the resurgence of militant fundamentalist Islam, of which the Iranian revolution is only the most obvious example. To a large extent this caught sociologists on the hop. Those who had predicted the Shah's downfall tended to assume that the impetus would be secular, progressive, possibly socialist. As it turned out, however, all those forces in Iranian society have received even shorter shrift than they did under the Shah from what is turning out to be a militant and deeply reactionary theocracy.

Evidently, millions of Iranians see the world in profoundly religious terms. They thus reacted to the Shah's 'modernization from above' not only as being politically dictatorial (which it was) and economically unsettling (which it also was), but above all as culturally alienating. The worst, it seems, that could be said – the symbol that had real power – was neither poverty nor tyranny as such, but *foreignness*. What is needed instead is a return to fundamentals; neither capitalism nor communism, but a truly Islamic development policy.

The fact that many Westerners find all this both puzzling and distasteful is no reason for not trying to understand it. Apart from showing up the tendency of secular-minded Western sociologists to downplay what they all too often regard as irrational religion, it is important to put Islamic fundamentalism in a broader context in two ways. Islam is not the only kind of fundamentalism around; and fundamentalism is not the only kind of Islam.

The fact that fundamentalist *Christianity* is also registering substantial gains (e.g. in East Asia, and parts of Latin America) suggests that a more general process is at work, in which people cling to unquestioned truths (albeit in revitalized forms) as a guiding thread in times of uncertainty and upheaval. Nor should one neglect the way religion can function as ideology. There is something in Marx's 'opium of the people' jibe, insofar as some forms of fundamentalism do deflect people's attention away from changing gross inequalities of power in this world.

Nonetheless, the note on which I want to end is to stress that in neither Islam nor Christianity do the fundamentalists go unchallenged. On the contrary, throughout their history the major world religions have functioned as 'terrains of meaning', subject to radically different interpretations and conflicts which may have profound social implications. Islam and Christianity alike have always had their reformers, their populists, their 'protestants'. Nor has this process ceased. In Iran today, the most active and persecuted oppositionists are a group called the Mojahedin; also devoutly Muslim, but with a reforming bent which stresses science and social progress (e.g. in the position of women, and the rights of minorities), and which regards Khomeini's brand of Islam as reactionary and indeed un-Islamic.

Similarly, within Christianity the Third World has found a distinctive voice in recent years in the form of 'liberation theology'. Originating in Latin America, where the Catholic Church had for long been regarded as a bastion of the *status quo*, liberation theology gives a very different slant: reading the Old Testament as a people's struggle against oppression, and the New Testament as the gospel of and for the poor and disinherited. As a result, radical Christians have become a politically important force in several countries, notably Nicaragua (where several priests serve in the Sandinista government, despite Vatican disapproval) and El Salvador (whose progressive Archbishop, Oscar Romero, was gunned down in his cathedral by right wingers).

In conclusion, it is perhaps ironic that while in the West (or North) sociologists debate the hypothesis of secularization, in the 'South' religious categories and identities seem to be as imbued with meaning as ever. This alone should be sufficient reason not to neglect this area. Naturally, it is never the province of sociologists to pronounce on the truth or falsity of religious claims. But in surveying religion in the Third World today, sociologists of development should not forget W. I. Thomas' famous axiom: if people think something is real, it *is* real in its consequences. In all its diverse forms – possible catalyst for development; categories for coping with upheavals caused by development; or terrains of meaning *within* which struggles take place – religion in the Third World is sociologically very real indeed.

Bibliography

Adamson, P. 'Global Report' (BBC2 TV, 31.12.1984)

Alavi, H. and Shanin, T. eds. *Introduction to the Sociology of the 'Developing Societies'* (Macmillan, London, 1982)

Amin, S. *Unequal Development* (Harvester, Hassocks, 1976)

Anderson, P. *Lineages of the Absolutist State* (New Left Books, London, 1974)

Arrighi, G. *The Political Economy of Rhodesia* (Mouton, The Hague, 1967)

Bairoch, P. *The Economic Development of the Third World since 1900* (Methuen, London, 1975)

Bernstein, H. ed. *Underdevelopment and Development* (Penguin, Harmondsworth, 1973)

Boserup, E. *Women's Role in Economic Development* (Allen & Unwin, London, 1970)

Brandt, W. *et al. North-South: a programme for Survival* (Pan, London, 1980)

Brenner, R. 'The origins of capitalist development: a critique of neo-Smithian Marxism' *New Left Review* 104, Jul–Aug. 1977

Bromley, R. ed. *The Urban Informal Sector: critical perspectives* (Pergamon, Oxford, 1978)

Bromley, R. and Gerry, C. eds. *Casual Work and Poverty in Third World Cities* (Wiley, Chichester, 1979)

Buchanan, K. *Reflections on Education in the Third World* (Spokesman, Nottingham, 1975)

Byres, T. J. and Crow, B. *The Green Revolution in India*. U204, case study 5. (Open University Press, Milton Keynes, 1983)

Cardoso, F. H. and Faletto, E. *Dependency and Development in Latin America* (University of California Press, Berkeley, 1979 (1971))

Carnoy, M. *Education as Cultural Imperialism* (Longman, London, 1974)

Chambers, R. *Rural Development: putting the last first* (Longman, London, 1983)

Cliffe, L. and Saul, J. eds. *Socialism in Tanzania: an interdisciplinary reader* 2 Vols (East African Publishing House, Nairobi, 1974)

Crow, B. and Thomas, A. *et al. Third World*

Atlas (Open University Press, Milton Keynes, 1983)

Dore, R. P. *The Diploma Disease: education, qualification, and development* (Allen & Unwin, London, 1976)

Dore, R. P. 'Making Sense of History' (Review of B. Moore) *European Journal of Sociology* Vol. X, No. 2, 1969

Elson, D. and Pearson, R. 'The Subordination of Women and the Internationalisation of Factory Production'. In K. Young *et al*, eds. *op. cit.*

Fanon, F. *The Wretched of the Earth* (Penguin, Harmondsworth, 1967)

Frank, A. G. *Capitalism and Underdevelopment in Latin America: historical studies of Chile and Brazil* (Monthly Review, New York, 1969a)

Frank, A. G. *Latin America: Underdevelopment or Revolution* (Monthly Review, New York, 1969b)

Freire, P. *Pedagogy of the Oppressed* (Penguin, Harmondsworth, 1975)

Furtado, C. *Development and Underdevelopment* (University of California Press, Berkeley, 1964)

Gerschenkron, A. *Economic Backwardness in Historical Perspective* (Harvard University Press, Cambridge, Mass, 1962)

Giele, J. Z. and Smock, A. C. eds. *Women: roles and status in eight countries* (Wiley, London, 1977)

Gilbert, A. and Gugler, J. *Cities, Poverty and Development: urbanization in the Third World* (Oxford University Press, Oxford, 1982)

Goldthorpe, J. E. *The Sociology of the Third World: disparity and development*, 2nd ed. (Cambridge University Press, Cambridge, 1984)

Hardiman, M. and Midgley, J. *The Social Dimensions of Development: social policy and planning in the Third World* (Wiley, Chichester, 1982)

Harrison, P. *Inside the Third World*, 2nd ed. (Penguin, Harmondsworth, 1981)

Haupt, A. and Kane, T. T. *Population Handbook: international edition* (Population Reference Bureau Inc, Washington DC, 1980)

Hilal, J. 'Sociology of Development' (Dept.

of Sociology, University of Durham, mimeo, 1970)

Hoogvelt, A. *The Sociology of Developing Societies* (Macmillan, London, 1976)

Hoogvelt, A. *The Third World in Global Development* (Macmillan, London, 1982)

Hoselitz, B. *Sociological Aspects of Economic Growth* (Free Press, Glencoe Ill., 1960)

Hyden, G. *Beyond Ujamaa in Tanzania: underdevelopment and an uncaptured peasantry* (Heinemann, London, 1980)

Illich, I. D. *Deschooling Society* (Penguin, Harmondsworth, 1975)

Johnson, H. 'Production on the Land'. Block 3, Part A of *Making a Living: production and producers on the land*. U204, Third World Studies (Open University Press, Milton Keynes, 1983)

Johnson, H. and Bernstein, H. eds. *Third World Lives of Struggle* (Heinemann, London, 1982)

Kahn, J. and Llobera, J. eds. *The Anthropology of Pre-Capitalist Societies* (Macmillan, London, 1981)

Kaplinsky, R. ed. *Third World Industrialization in the 1980s: open economies in a closing world* (Cass, London, 1984) Also available as *Journal of Development Studies*, Vol. 21, No. 1, Oct. 1984

Kemp, T. *Industrialization in the Non-Western World* (Longman, London, 1983)

Kirkpatrick, C. H. and Nixson, F. I. eds. *The Industrialization of Less Developed Countries* (Manchester University Press, Manchester, 1983)

Kitching, G. *Development and Underdevelopment in Historical Perspective: populism, nationalism and industrialization* (Methuen, London, 1982)

Kerr, C. *et al. Industrialism and Industrial Man* (Heinemann, London, 1962)

Kumar, K. *Prophecy and Progress* (Penguin, Harmondsworth, 1978)

Laclau, E. 'Feudalism and Capitalism in Latin America' *New Left Review*, 67, May–June, 1971

Lea, D. A. M. and Chaudhri, D. P. eds. *Rural Development and the State: contradictions and dilemmas in developing countries* (Methuen, London, 1983)

Lee, D. and Newby, H. *The Problem of Sociology* (Hutchinson, London, 1983)

Lewis, O. *La Vida: a Puerto Rican family in the culture of poverty* (Panther, London, 1969)

Lipton, M. *Why Poor People Stay Poor: urban bias in world development* (Temple Smith, London, 1977)

Lloyd, P. *Slums of Hope?* (Penguin, Harmondsworth, 1979)

Long, N. *An Introduction to the Sociology of Rural Development* (Tavistock, London, 1977)

Love, J. L. 'Third World: a response to Professor Worsley' *Third World Quarterly* Vol. II, No. 2, Apr. 1980

MacPherson, S. *Social Policy in the Third World: the social dilemmas of underdevelopment* (Wheatsheaf, Brighton, 1982)

Mamdani, M. *The Myth of Population Control: family, caste and class in an Indian village* (Monthly Review, New York, 1972)

Michaelson, K. L. *And the Poor Get Children: radical perspectives on population dynamics* (Monthly Review, New York, 1981)

Molyneux, M. 'Women in Socialist Societies: problems of theory and practice'. In K. Young, *et al.* eds. *op. cit.*

Moore, B. Jr. *Social Origins of Dictatorship and Democracy: lord and peasant in the making of the modern world* (Penguin, Harmondsworth, 1966)

Myrdal, G. *Economic Theory and Underdeveloped Regions* (Methuen, London, 1963)

Nash, J. and Safa H. E. eds. *Sex and Class in Latin America* (Praeger, London, 1976)

Nisbet, R. *The Sociological Tradition* (Heinemann, London, 1967)

Open University *U204: Third World Studies*, 5 blocks in 8 volumes, 10 'case studies' atlas, and other materials; various authors (Open University Press, Milton Keynes, 1983)

Oxaal, I., Barnett, A. and Booth, D. eds. *Beyond the Sociology of Development* (Routledge & Kegan Paul, London, 1975)

Palmer, R. and Parsons, N. eds. *The Roots of Rural Poverty in Central and Southern Africa* (Heinemann, London, 1977)

Redclift, M. *Development and the Environmental Crisis: red and green alternatives* (Methuen, London, 1984)

Roberts, B. *Cities of Peasants* (Arnold, London, 1978)

Rodney, W. *How Europe Underdeveloped Africa* (Bogle-L'Ouverture, London, 1972)

Rogers, B. *The Domestication of Women: discrimination in developing societies* (Kogan Page, London, 1980)

Rohrlich-Leavitt, R. ed. *Women Cross-Culturally: change and challenge* (Mouton, The Hague, 1975)

Rostow, W. W. *The Stages of Economic Growth: a non-communist manifesto*, 2nd ed. (Cambridge University Press, Cambridge, 1971) (1960)

Roxborough, I. *Theories of Underdevelopment* (Macmillan, London, 1979)

Rweyemamu, J. F. *et al. Towards Socialist Planning* (Tanzania Publishing House, Dar es Salaam, 1974)

Saffiotti, H. I. B. *Women in Class Society* (Monthly Review, New York, 1978)

Sandbrook, R. *The Politics of Basic Needs: urban aspects of assaulting poverty in Africa* (Heinemann, London, 1982)

Schumacher, E. F. *Small is Beautiful* (Sphere, London, 1974)

Seers, D. 'The limitations of the special case' In *The Teaching of Development Economics*, edited by K. Martin and J. Knapp (Cass, London, 1967)

Shanin, T. ed. *Peasants and Peasant Societies* (Penguin, Harmondsworth, 1971)

Skocpol, T. *States and Social Revolutions* (Cambridge University Press, Cambridge, 1979)

Sutcliffe, R. B. *Industry and Underdevelopment* (Addison-Wesley, London, 1971)

Szentes, T. ' "Status Quo" and Socialism', Ch. 71 in Cliffe and Saul eds. *op. cit.*

Taylor, J. *From Modernization to Modes of Production: a critique of the sociologies of development and underdevelopment* (Macmillan, London, 1979)

Thomas, A. 'Third World: images, definitions, connotations'. In *The 'Third World' and 'Development'* U204, Third World Studies, Block 1 (Open University Press, Milton Keynes, 1983)

Thomas, C. Y. *Dependence and Transformation* (Monthly Review, New York, 1974)

Turner, J. F. C. *Housing By People* (Marion Boyars, London, 1976)

Vogeler, I. and De Souza, A. *Dialectics of Third World Development* (Allanheld, Osmun & Co. Totowa, N.J., 1980)

Wade, R. and White G. eds. 'Developmental States in East Asia: capitalist and socialist' *IDS Bulletin*, Vol. 15, No. 2, Apr. 1984

Wallerstein, I. *The Capitalist World Economy* (Cambridge University Press, Cambridge, 1979)

Warren, B. *Imperialism: Pioneer of Capitalism* (New Left Books/Verso, London, 1980)

Webster, A. *Introduction to the Sociology of Development* (Macmillan, London, 1984)

White, C. P. 'Socialist transformation of agriculture and gender relations: the Vietnamese Case' *IDS Bulletin*, Vol. 13, No. 4, Sep. 1982

Wield, D. 'Industrial Production: Factories and Workers' In *Making a Living: production and producers in the Third World*, Block 3, Parts B–C. U204, Third World Studies (Open University Press, Milton Keynes, 1983)

Williamson, B. *Education, Social Structure and Development: a comparative analysis* (Macmillan, London, 1979)

(World Bank) *World Development Report* Various years (World Bank, Washington, DC)

Worsley, P. 'How Many Worlds?' *Third World Quarterly*, Vol. I, No. 2, April, 1979

Young, K. *et al.* eds. *Of Marriage and the Market: women's subordination in international perspective* (CSE Books, London, 1981)

Index

nature 42
neolithic 69
new international division of labour 34–37
New Zealand 4
newly industrializing countries (NICs) 19,
    31–37, 117
Nicaragua 10, 88, 99, 120
Nigeria 93
Nisbet, R. 26, 39
North/South 4
Notestein, F. 71
Nyerere, J. 98

Oil 8, 41
Ottoman empire 8

Pakistan 8
Palestine 103
Pan-Africanism 7
Panslavists 102
Papua New Guinea 101
Paraguay 18
pattern variables 22
peasantization 60–61
peasants 24, 49, 57–67, 76
peasant culture 59, 60, 61
peasant mode of production 65
peasant politics 62–63
Peru 10, 36, 85, 87
petty commodity producers 49
Philippines 9
physical quality of life index (PQLI) 5
pollution 40–41
Pol Pot 9
population 7, 9, 10, 44–45, 53, 65, 68–77
Portugal 9, 37
Post, K. 60
Prebisch, R. 29
preventive/curative medicine 79, 85–86, 90
primate city 46
production 5
proletarianization 52, 57, 64
proletariat 20, 24
protectionism 30, 34
Protestant Ethic 23, 33, 116–117
psychologism 22–23
public/private 107
Puerto Rico 50
Punjab 9, 64, 74, 110
purdah 107

raw materials 7, 8, 9, 10, 28
recapitulation 11, 15, 27, 45–47, 73, 82, 90

red/school 102
Redfield, R. 59–60
religion 116–120
resources 41, 71
revolution 23–25
Ricardo, D. 28
ritual 56
Roberts, B. 58
Rodney, W. 3
Rogers, B. 105–106
Roman Catholicism 68, 73, 120
Rome 44
Romero 120
Roots 93
Rostow, W. W. 12–16, 22
rural development 53–67, 82, 105–106

Saffiotti, H. 108
Sahel 55
Sandinista 120
Saudi Arabia 8, 103
Schumacher, E. F. 40
science 13–14, 63–65, 79–80
Scotland 100
secularization 120
Senegal 102
Shah 119
Shanin, T. 58–62
shanty-towns 49–51
sharecropping 54, 57, 59, 64
Sikhs 65
Silvey, J. 98–99
Singapore 33, 37, 45, 117
Singh, K. 75
skill 111
Skocpol, T. 25
slavery 7, 10
socialism 20, 112–113
social mobility 21, 36, 96, 106
solidarity, mechanical/organic 22
Somalia 99, 112
South Africa 7, 102, 108, 118
South Yemen 112
Spain 9
Spencer, H. 3
spontaneous settlements 50
Sri Lanka 5, 8, 88, 98
stage theories 3, 13–16, 22
stagnationism 18–19, 32
Stalin, J. V. 62
state 16, 30, 31, 36, 49, 69, 75–76
    and peasants 60, 65–66
strategies 28–37